はじめに

More Outstanding Brochures, Catalogues and Pamphlets from Across the Business Spectrum

Catalog & Pamphlet Collection

vol.3

P·I·E BOOKS

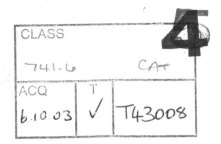
Catalog & Pamphlet Collection vol.3

P·I·E BOOKS

Villa Phoenix Suite 301, 4-14-6,
Komagome, Toshima-ku, Tokyo 170-0003 Japan
Phone: +81-3-3940-8302 Fax: +81+3-3576-7361

Please note our change of contact details from 17th march 2003.
2-32-4, Minami-Otsuka, Toshima-ku, Tokyo 170-0005 Japan
Phone: +81-3-5395-4811 Fax: +81-3-5395-4812

e-mail: editor@piebooks.com
        sales@piebooks.com
http://www.piebooks.com

ISBN 4-89444-239-6 C3070
Printed in Japan

本書は好評につき完売した「ブローシャーアンドパンフレットコレクション4」の改訂版です。
序文は上記タイトルのために書かれたものをそのまま使用しています。

This book was previously published in a popular hardcover edition entitled
"A Brochure and Pamphlet Collection 4."
References to the title in the foreword of hence reflect the original title.

CONTENTS

情報があふれる現在、消費者はより明確で、それぞれの感性
にあった、上質な情報だけを選び取るようになってきています。
ある意味で、情報に対しても、物に対しても、以前より貪欲にな
ってきたと言えるのではないでしょうか。

　購入する、ということをとってみても、その商品が自分の生活
スタイルに本当にあっているものなのかどうかなどをゆっくり
と吟味し、そして、自分にとって本当に必要だと思うものだけ
を購入するようになってきているように思います。

　"本当に必要なもの"いってみればとてもシンプルなことなの
ですが、必要と決めるまでにはさまざまなプロセスがあります。
その商品のイメージ、色、材質・素材、値段などを吟味し、その
商品と値段が本当に見合ったものなのかどうかをじっくり考え
たり...。そしてまた、その考え悩むということも、購入する際
の大切な要素であり、楽しみのひとつなのです。

　今回で第4弾になる本書"ブローシュア アンド パンフレッ
ト"シリーズですが、消費者がますます貪欲になっていくにつ
れ、デザインの観点からも、少しずつ変わってきているように
思います。

　以前では、イメージばかりが先行してしまっていたものや、感
覚的過ぎて商品がよくわからないものが多く見られたように思
いますが、今では、商品のディテール・素材感がよく分かり、
ヴィジュアル的にも、感覚的にも調和のとれた、それでいてク
ライアントの、デザイナーの、個性あふれる作品が楽しめるよ
うになりました。

　本書でも、そんな素晴らしい作品ばかりを集め、ファッショ
ン／アクセサリー／コスメティック／流通・販売／スポーツ／
乗物／電気製品／食品・飲料／家具・生活用品／建築関連／音
楽・映像／イベントと、今を代表する各業種別に分類し、それ
ぞれのデザイン傾向が一覧できるようにしました。また、作品
の豊かな表情をお楽しみ頂けるよう、1ページ1作品を基本に、
表紙から中ページまでを掲載しています。ご覧いただく皆様に、
作品のリアル感がより効果的にお伝えできれば幸いです。

　最後に、本書にために貴重な作品をお送り下さいました皆様、
ならびに制作に当たりご協力いただきました皆様に心より
お礼を申し上げます。

P・I・E BOOKS 編集部

FOREWORD

Deluged these days by information, the average consumer is getting increasingly selective and prefers informative material that is high in quality, comprehensible, and speaks to his or her particular sensitivities. But it may perhaps be true to say that consumers have a greater hunger for information and for goods than ever before.

Before making a purchase, people take the time to find out whether the article is really suited to their lifestyle and seem to buy only those things they deem essential. An 'essential item' may be a simple enough concept, but deciding that something is indeed essential involves a complex process. The image associated with the article, its color, material and price all have to be considered, as well as whether or not it is really value for money. The effort put into the decision is one important element of the purchase and part of its pleasure.

As we believe this fourth edition of our 'Brochure and Pamphlets' series shows, the trend towards consumers becoming more and more hungry for information is paralleled by changes in design trends for promotional brochures.

Previously, all too often image was everything, or else the design was so esoteric the product was all but invisible. But now the feel and the detailed styling of the product are made very clear, visual balance is achieved and a sense of the individuality of client or designer comes through strongly.

This volume is a selection of the very best artwork for this type of promotional material. It covers many business areas, ranging from fashion-related products to food and drink, electrical equipment, household goods, and events and entertainments, arranged to show at a glance recent design trends in each of these categories. As far as possible, one page is given over to each sample of artwork and both cover and inside pages are shown, to allow a thorough appreciation of the integrated design. We hope that this approach will give readers a better overall idea of the pamphlets and brochures the book features.

Finally, we would like to offer our thanks to all those who kindly contributed artwork for this publication and

CREDIT FORMAT

Client
クライアント名

Type of Company / 業種

Intended Use / 使用目的

Year of Completion 制作年度

A: Agency

PR: Producer

CD: Creative Director

CC: Creative Coordinator

AD: Art Director

D: Designer

P: Photographer

CW: Copywriter

I: Illustrator

O: Object

HM: Hair and Make-up

S: Stylist

DF: Design Firm

PD: Printing Director

EDITORIAL NOTES

ONWARD KASHIYAMA CO., LTD.

㈱オンワード樫山

Apparel maker / アパレル メーカー
Product catalogue / 製品案内
1995
CD: Paul Smith
AD: Alan Aboud
P: Julian Broad
size: 364×520 mm

Fashion

• **NAIGAI CO., LTD.**

㈱ナイガイ

Apparel maker / アパレル メーカー
Product catalogue / 製品案内
1995
CD: Fendissime Co., Ltd.
P: Craig McDean
size: 190×148 mm

Pct page: T-SHIRT no.4300/43 ¥6,900 cream, khaki, chocolatebrown, black
SHORTS no.725778 ¥1,700 beige, black SOCKS sample
opposite page: BRASSIERE no.70142 ¥3,400 white

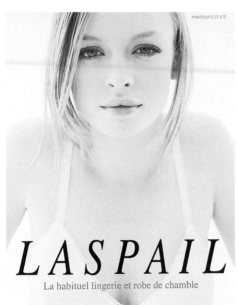

PRINTEMPS ET ÉTÉ

LASPAIL

La habituel lingerie et robe de chamble

Pct page: SHIRT no.434424 ¥6,900 khaki, chocolatebrown, black
SLIP no.525776 ¥7,900 beige, black
opposite page: CAMISOLE no.539873 ¥5,900 offwhite, beige, mochabrown, black
SHORTS no.725678 ¥5,900 offwhite, beige, mochabrown, black
CUSHION no.334306 ¥5,900 offwhite, lilac, cream, black

Pct page: ONE-PIECE no.334605 ¥6,900 beige, green, chocolatebrown, black
opposite page: JAKET no.412711 ¥9,900 white, beige, indigoblue
PANTS no.412712 ¥6,900 white, beige, indigoblue

BE SQUARE CO., LTD. •

㈱ビー スクエア

Apparel maker / アパレル メーカー
Product catalogue / 製品案内
1995
CD: Chizuko Murao　村尾 千鶴子
AD, D: Hiroko Tanuma　田沼広子
P: Masashi Ohashi　大橋聖史
size: 277×210 mm

Fashion • 013

• **F CO., LTD.**

㈱エフ

Apparel maker / アパレル メーカー
Product catalogue / 製品案内
1991
CD: Yoshiyuki Shimazu　島津由行
AD, D: Yuka Kubota　久保田 友加
P: Naoki Tsuruta / Nanako Sato
鶴田直樹 / サトウ ナナコ
size: 364×260 mm

MORGAN FISHER（アーティスト）

どうも、近頃、世の中ヒステリックだ。エイズ、戦争、麻薬、そして民族と宗教問題。特にお金に絡むニュースには、もうウンザリするばかり。火山が噴火しても善良で非力な市民ばかりが被害にあう。悪い奴には天罰と言うものがなかなか下らない。それどころか「悪い奴程、よく眠る」なんて大ウソで、奴等は、酒も飲まなきゃ煙草も吸わず、高級会員制アスレチックで体調を整え、超一流ホテルの朝食ミーティングに集まっては、弱い者いじめを画策している。エコロジーを謳う企業が、実は公害の元凶パワー・ウォーズの旗手であったり、リサイクル物がオリジナル物より高かったり、元来人間の本質にふれる「ファジー」を、家電の代名詞にしたりして…でも文句は言えないかも知れない。そうでしょ、回りを見渡してもSEXと財テクにしか興味がない人が多過ぎるもの。「水」と「サービス」はタダといまだに思い込んでいるような人が、臭いオシボリで顔を拭きながら「日本は、ソフトに対する認識が低すぎる」なんて発言するんだから。僕は「まっ、いいか」この一言で80年代を乗り切った。それは「本質」ではなく「本格」の時代であったから。本格的○○料理（エスニックを含めて）、本格的スポーツ・カー、本格的オペラ（ミュージカルを含めて）…何でもお金に任せて「本格」と呼ばれるものを出前してもらえばよかったのだから。ただ、いかんせん、いくら本格と言えども、出前だけにその奥行きには限界があった。この奥行きの限界を垣間見た人達は、新たなる価値感を求め出した。それは、外に向けてではなく、自己の内なる幸せ充足感に向けて静かに、しかし確実に価値感に対する意識の転化が行われている。ブロードウェイミュージカルは、ビッグアップルに行って観るものだ。アウト・バーンのない国で、300km/hの車の話は、童話の様に素直に受け入れるもので、東名と比較してはいけない。料理は材料によって貪欲に変化することにより芸術性を持つもので、パリとの味の違いがわかっても、何にも偉くないのだ。僕にとっての本質とは、いつ、どこで、誰と何を、どんな気分で過ごすのか…それしかない。もう一言付け加えるなら、その一瞬をより高揚させる為に何が要るのか。そしてその選び方の哲学を自分が持ち得ているのか、それが問題だ。やはり「本質」と「自己」とは背中合せなのだ。

• **TSUKAMOTO CO., LTD.**
  NEVERLAND DIV.

ツカモト㈱ ネバーランド事業部

Apparel maker / アパレル メーカー

Product catalogue / 製品案内

1994

CD: Chizuko Murao　村尾 千鶴子

AD, D: Masashi Hisasue　久末正史

P: Karel Fonteyne

size: 297×210 mm

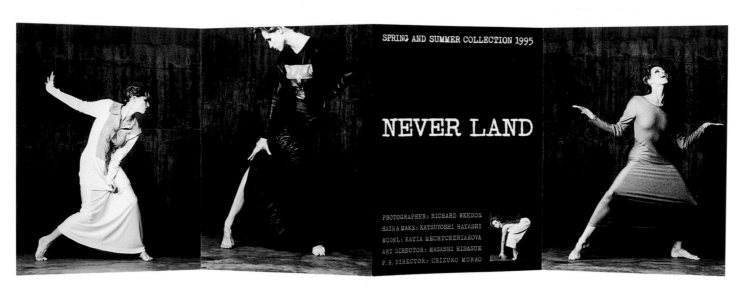

SPRING AND SUMMER COLLECTION 1995

NEVER LAND

PHOTOGRAPHER: RICHARD WEEDON
HAIR & MAKE: KATSUYOSHI HAYASHI
MODEL: KATIA MECHTCHERIAKOVA
ART DIRECTOR: MASASHI HISASUE
P. R. DIRECTOR: CHIZUKO MURAO

**TSUKAMOTO CO., LTD. •
NEVERLAND DIV.**

ツカモト㈱ ネバーランド事業部

Apparel maker / アパレル メーカー
Product catalogue / 製品案内
1995
CD: Chizuko Murao　村尾 千鶴子
AD, D: Masashi Hisasue　久末正史
P: Richard Weedon
size: 257×190 mm

Fashion • 017

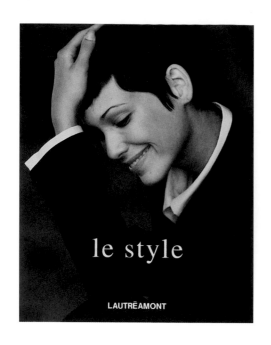

le style

LAUTRÉAMONT

• LAUTRÉAMONT CO., LTD.

㈱ロートレアモン

Apparel maker / アパレル メーカー

Product catalogue / 製品案内

1993

CD, AD: Shuji Horiguchi　堀口秀司

D: Junko Otsuka　大塚順子

P: Hisashi Shimizu / Hiroto Ishiwata

清水 尚 / 石渡洋人

CW: Motoko Hayashi　林 元子

size: 285×220 mm

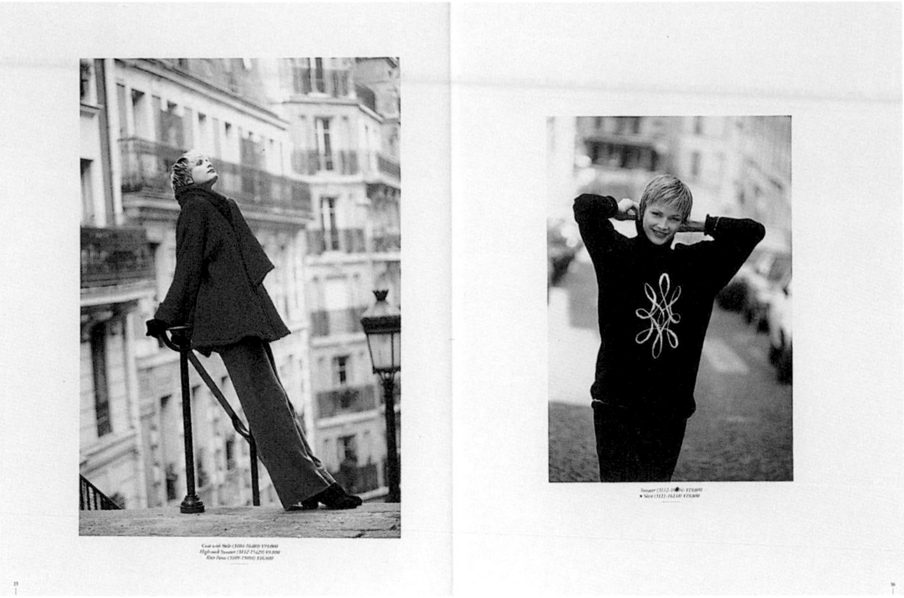

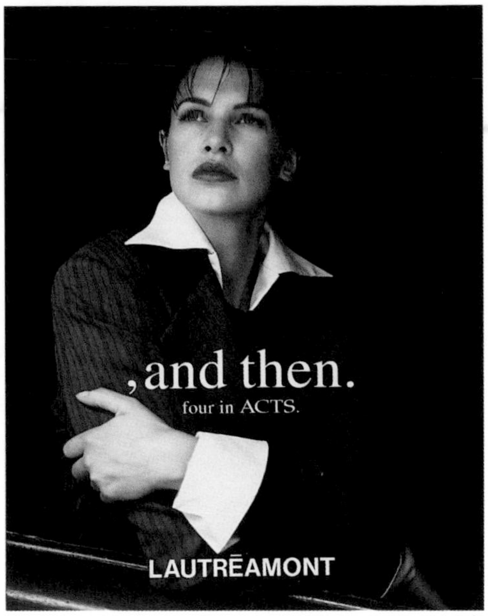

, and then.
four in ACTS.
LAUTRĒAMONT

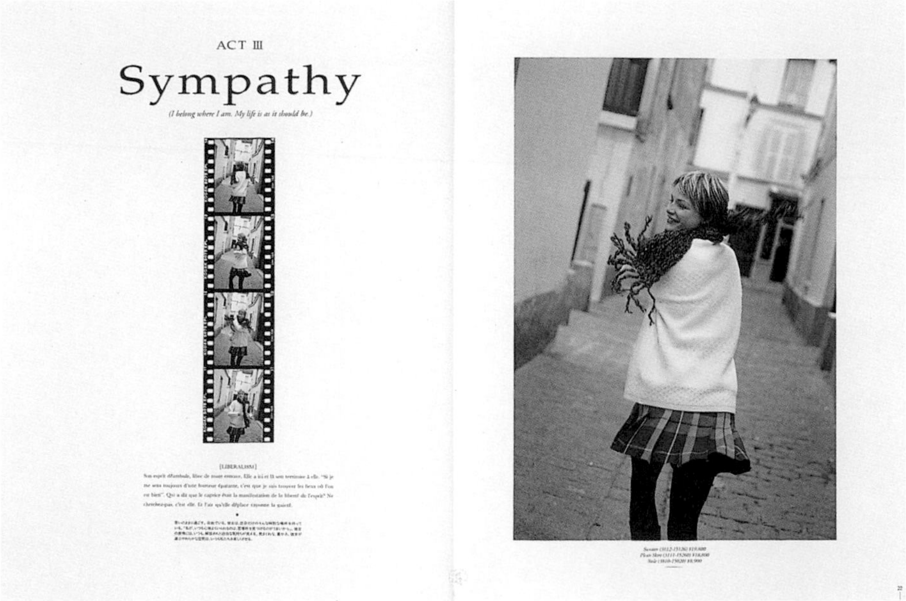

ACT III
Sympathy

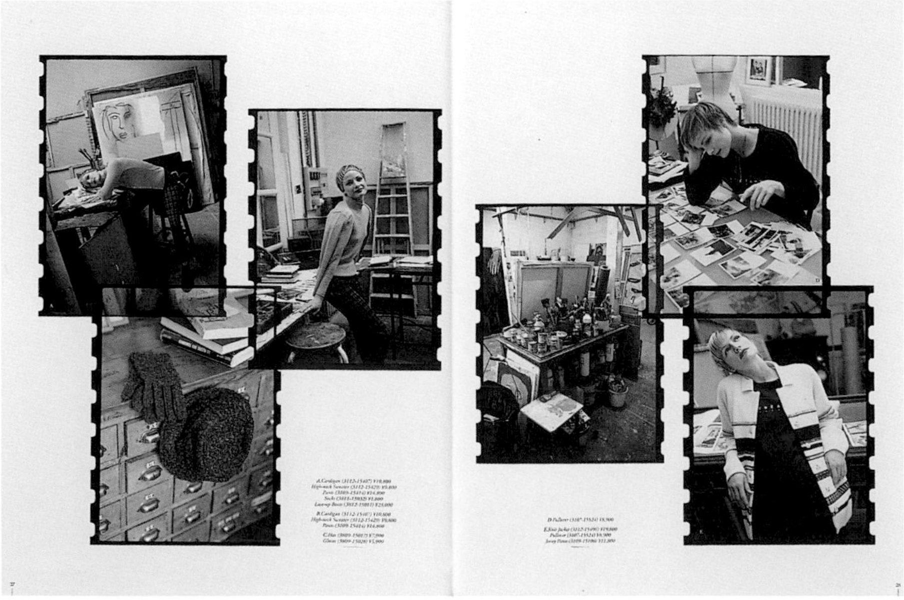

LAUTRÉAMONT CO., LTD. •

㈱ロートレアモン

Apparel maker / アパレル メーカー

Product catalogue / 製品案内

1994

CD, AD: Shuji Horiguchi 堀口秀司

D: Junko Otsuka 大塚順子

P: Hisashi Shimizu / Hiroto Ishiwata

清水 尚 / 石渡洋人

CW: Motoko Hayashi 林 元子

size: 285×220 mm

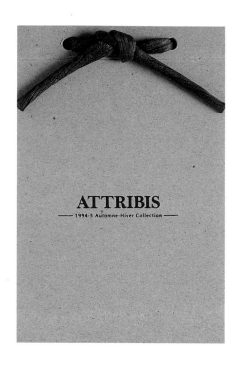

● **LAUTRÉAMONT CO., LTD.**
㈱ロートレアモン

Apparel maker / アパレル メーカー
Product catalogue / 製品案内
1994
CD, AD: Shuji Horiguchi　堀口秀司
D: Junko Otsuka　大塚順子
P: Masaki Oda　小田雅樹
size: 160×105 mm

1995 PRINTEMPS COLLECTION 渡辺洋人

L

LAUTRĒAMONT

LAUTRÉAMONT CO., LTD. •

㈱ロートレアモン

Apparel maker / アパレル メーカー

Product catalogue / 製品案内

1995

CD, AD: Shuji Horiguchi　堀口秀司

D: Yukiyo Kaneko　金子幸代

P: Hiroto "Kiriu" Ishiwata　石渡洋人

size: 110×80 mm

Fashion • 021

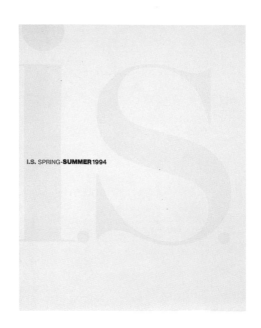

I.S. SPRING-**SUMMER** 1994

ISSEY MIYAKE INC.
イッセイミヤケ㈱

Apparel maker / アパレル メーカー
Product catalogue / 製品案内
1994
CD: Yoshiyuki Shimazu　島津由行
AD, D: Yuka Kubota　久保田 友加
P: Shunsuke Kuboki　久保木 浚介
size: 297×230 mm

45RPM STUDIO CO., LTD. •

フォーティーファイブ アールピーエム㈱

Apparel maker / アパレル メーカー

Product catalogue / 製品案内

1995

CD: Chizuko Murao　村尾 千鶴子

AD, D: Junichi Aso　麻生順一

P: Noboru Kikuchi　菊地　昇

size: 330×265 mm

Fashion • 023

When you feel it, touch it, see it, belive it and find it ············

• **45RPM STUDIO CO., LTD.**
フォーティーファイブ アールピーエム㈱

Apparel maker / アパレル メーカー
Product catalogue / 製品案内
1994
AD, D: Joji Yano　矢野譲二
P: Ryoichi Takahashi　高橋良一
size: 297×210 mm

45RPM STUDIO CO., LTD. •

フォーティーファイブ アールピーエム㈱

Apparel maker / アパレル メーカー

Product catalogue / 製品案内

1994

AD, D: Joji Yano　矢野譲二

P: Ryoichi Takahashi　高橋良一

size: 297×210 mm

Fashion • 025

- **BIGI CO., LTD.**
  ㈱ビギ

  Apparel maker / アパレル メーカー
  Product catalogue / 製品案内
  1995
  CD, AD, D: Bigi Co., Ltd.　㈱ビギ
  P: Itaru Hirama　平間 至
  HM: Katsuya Kamo (Mod's Hair)
  加茂克也（モッズ・ヘアー）
  size: 257×183 mm

"Elle est cool.
Elle est branchée.
Elle est exotique.
Elle est libérée.
Elle fait sensation.
Elle est vraiment remarquable…
Car elle est la mode totale."

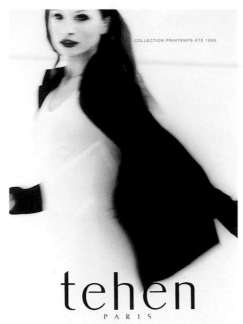

COLLECTION PRINTEMPS-ÉTÉ 1995

tehen
PARIS

Quoi De Neuf?

Actuel. Un Style Séduisant. Libéré. Agréable. Des Petits Tee-Shirts. Des Coloris Accentués.

ITOKIN CO., LTD. •

イトキン㈱

Apparel maker / アパレル メーカー

Product catalogue / 製品案内

1995

CD, AD: Shuji Horiguchi　堀口秀司

D: Yukiyo Kaneko　金子幸代

P: Masaki Oda　小田雅樹

CW: Motoko Hayashi　林　元子

size: 364×260 mm

Fashion • 027

• **SCANLAN & THEODORE**

Apparel maker / アパレル メーカー

Product catalogue / 製品案内

1993

AD, D: Andrew Hoyne

P: Ross Bird

CW: Kristina Garla

DF: Andrew Hoyne Design

size: 210×145 mm

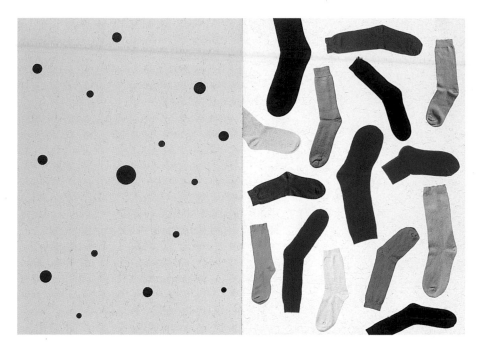

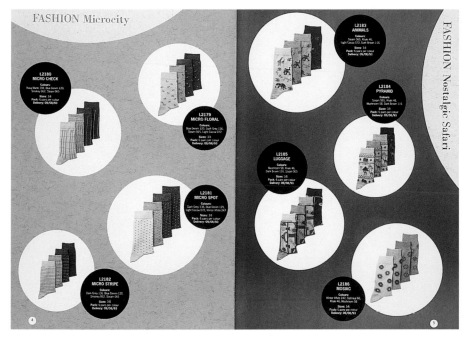

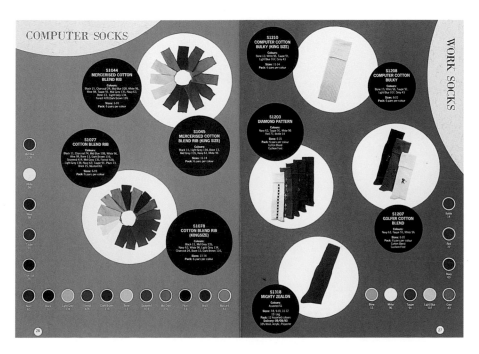

HOLEPROOF •

Apparel maker / アパレル メーカー

Product catalogue / 製品案内

1993

AD: Andrew Hoyne

P: Rob Blackburn

DF: Andrew Hoyne Design

size: 302×218 mm

Fashion • 029

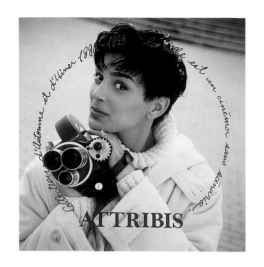

• **LAUTRÉAMONT CO., LTD.**

㈱ロートレアモン

Apparel maker / アパレル メーカー
Product catalogue / 製品案内
1992
CD, AD: Shuji Horiguchi　堀口秀司
D: Junko Otsuka　大塚順子
P: Masaki Oda　小田雅樹
CW: Motoko Hayashi　林　元子
size: 220×210 mm

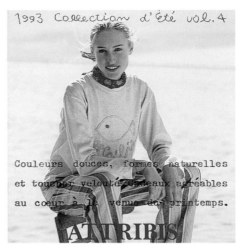

LAUTRÉAMONT CO., LTD. •

㈱ロートレアモン

Apparel maker / アパレル メーカー

Product catalogue / 製品案内

1993

CD, AD: Shuji Horiguchi　堀口秀司

D: Junko Otsuka　大塚順子

P: Masaki Oda　小田雅樹

CW: Motoko Hayashi　林　元子

size: 220×210 mm

Fashion • 031

1993 JEANS COLLECTION
SOMETHING

En général, je vais au lycée en vélo. Les rues de Paris sont souvent pavées et je suis secouée mais ça ne me dérange pas. Mon style le plus fréquent des jeans, une veste en daim et un béret. Pour les jeans, je préfère des pantalons droits resserrés vers les chevilles pour que les mouvements de mes jambes soient plus naturels. Ce matin, j'ai mis un pullover couleur café au lait. Dans les cafés, les garçons ont l'air très occupé aux préparatifs du matin. La lumière douce du matin et l'animation des gens. J'aime ce moment où je me dis, encore une journée qui commence. Bonjour ! Bonjour ! Bonjour ! Je veux dire bonjour avec un grand sourire à tous ceux que je rencontre.

• **EDWIN CO., LTD.**

エドウィン

Apparel maker / アパレル メーカー

Product catalogue / 製品案内

1992

CD: Kenji Suzuki　鈴木賢二

AD: Kazuko Mizunuma　水沼和子

D: Akiko Shigeto　重藤明子

P: Yoshinori Onda　恩田義則

CW: Toru Kawanishi　河西　亨

DF: Permanent., Inc.　パーマネント・インク

size: 297×210 mm

L'endroit le plus sympa en ce moment: le quartier de la Bastille à Paris. Et puis les Halles peut-être. A la Bastille, il y a les discos les plus branchées et des salles de billard, et le week-end tout le quartier est peuplé de jeunes. Aux Halles, je suis souvent faire du shopping avec une amie. Il y a beaucoup de boutiques de vêtements marrants et pas chers. Aujourd'hui, j'ai rendez-vous avec mon petit ami à Saint Germain. Un quartier plus adulte et élégant. Je me suis habillée façon Western, avec un jean en denim noir super confortable et une veste à franges. Les Something sont de rigueur cette tenue et c'est la grande mode en ce moment chez les jeunes Parisiennes de se vêtir en cow-boy.

*t*urquoise

ターコイズシリーズはサムシングブランドのなかでいちばん
基本のベーシックツインいわば基本シリーズです。
スリムとストレート、はっきりとしたシルエットのバリエーションが揃っているので
自分に似合うシリーズが見つかります。
2色のあいなるアイテムばかりなので、その年のシーンで活躍するアイテムを、
フロントボタンに特徴のあるターコイズが、目印です。

ターコイズ・ヒドゥ A・カート3個ポケットシートパンツ（ロゴT：8081-081）フリンウォッシュ ¥4,200
ジーンズ LOT.8031（ブラック）¥5,300

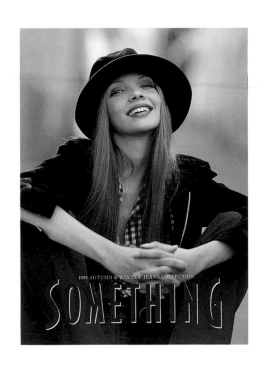

1993 AUTUMN & WINTER JEANS COLLECTION
SOMETHING

*O*ther bottoms

サムシングブランドには基本のボトッ外シリーズのほかにもいろいろ
多彩なアイテムがあります。
豊富なカラー・バリエーションのルーズ・ストレートからモノズ・カーメント・ワークスのオール
多彩なランナップがそろっています。日本のあらゆるシーンで活躍するアイテムを、その年のシーンに合うものを1グッムを選んでください。

レギュラートラウザー LOT.8031-0401 '97 ¥2,200
シューズ LOT.8051（ブラック）¥15,800

カラー・ルーミーストレート（ゆったりストレート161）LOT.9071-07（ソフトブラウン）¥7,900

カラー・ルーミーストレート [ゆったりストレート 04]	ルーミーストレート [ゆったりストレート 04]

02	08	47	27	17	74	86	73
24							

レギュラートラウザー	オーセンティック・トラウザー

04	14	36	47	04	14	36	76

J'ai décidé de ne pas être ronchon. C'est ma devise. Bien sûr ce
n'est pas toujours facile, mais j'essaie de n'y tenir. Je pense que
les gens qui ronchonnent tout le temps ne sont pas très intéressants. Et les gens qui parlent en geignant
ne sont pas très intéressants. Et les gens qui pensent trop au qui
prennent tout trop au sérieux, c'est fatigant! J'aime les gens qui
sont légers, et qui sourient. Parce que ce n'est pas possible d'être
en parfaite harmonie avec quelqu'un. Il y a toujours quelques
millimètres de différence. C'est pour cela que tout va bien mieux
si on se fréquente en mettant une certaine distance, un certain
relâchement entre nous. Et puis ce qui est responsable de ses
pareils. C'est une très bonne chose que de pouvoir oublier.

EDWIN CO., LTD. •

エドウィン

Apparel maker / アパレル メーカー

Product catalogue / 製品案内

1993

CD: Kenji Suzuki　鈴木賢二

AD: Kazuko Mizunuma　水沼和子

D: Akiko Shigeto　重藤明子

P: Masanobu Seike　清家正信

CW: Toru Kawanishi　河西 亨

DF: Permanent., Inc.　パーマネント・インク

size: 297×210 mm

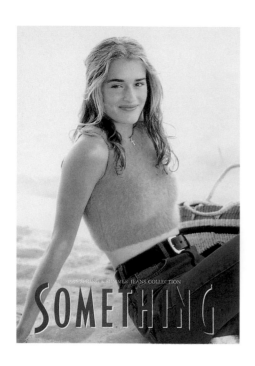

1995 SPRING & SUMMER JEANS COLLECTION

SOMETHING

TURQUOISE

WORK

FLARE PANTS,
TIGHT STRAIGHT, SLENDER PANTS

- **EDWIN CO., LTD.**

エドウィン

Apparel maker / アパレル メーカー

Product catalogue / 製品案内

1994

CD: Kenji Suzuki　鈴木賢二

AD: Kazuko Mizunuma　水沼和子

D: Akiko Shigeto　重藤明子

P: Yoshinori Onda　恩田義則

CW: Toru Kawanishi　河西 亨

DF: Permanent., Inc.　パーマネント・インク

size: 297×210 mm

EDWIN CO., LTD. •

エドウィン

Apparel maker / アパレル メーカー

Product catalogue / 製品案内

1995

AD, D: Yasushi Nakayama 中山 泰

DF: NYC

size: 594×450 mm

Fashion • 035

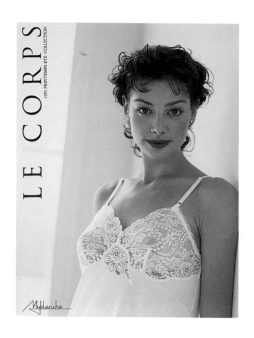

MY BRANCHE

㈱マイブランシュ

Apparel maker / 下着メーカー

Product catalogue / 製品案内

1995

CD: Jun-ichi Furuyama　古山準一

AD: Mikio Ioka　井岡幹夫

D: Rie Honda　本多利江

P: Jiro Fujimura　藤村治郎

CW: Michiko Kawai / Mika Takeshita

川井道子 / 竹下美香

DF: Alphad　㈱アルファード

size: 297×230 mm

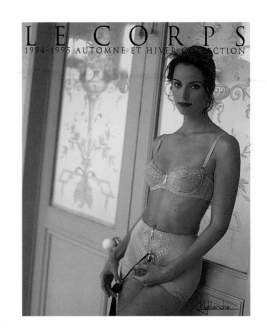

LE CORPS
1994-1995 AUTOMNE ET HIVER COLLECTION

Soft Impression

やすらかな、出会い。

When you wake up from a good night's sleep and get the feeling that you'll meet someone, you begin to feel the tension in your mind, in your body. That's a precious morning for any woman.

Sera THREE

Adore ZONE

A n idle afternoon all for myself! Wouldn't it be nice to walk through the subtle trees. Wouldn't it be wonderful to open a book one is reading. Wrapped gently and naturally. I want to spend the afternoon like a fresh and honest little girl.

MY BRANCHE •

㈱マイブランシュ

Apparel maker / 下着メーカー

Product catalogue / 製品案内

1994

CD: Jun-ichi Furuyama　古山準一

AD: Mikio Ioka　井岡幹夫

D: Rie Honda　本多利江

P: Jiro Fujimura　藤村治郎

CW: Michiko Kawai / Mika Takeshita

川井道子 / 竹下美香

DF: Alphad　㈱アルファード

size: 297×230 mm

Fashion • 037

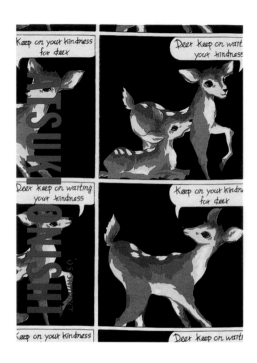

• **P / X CO., LTD.**

㈱ピー・エックス

Apparel maker / アパレル メーカー

Product catalogue / 製品案内

1995

size: 297×210 mm

Chéri LEOPARD FAIR Mon Chéri LEOPARD FAIR Mon Chéri

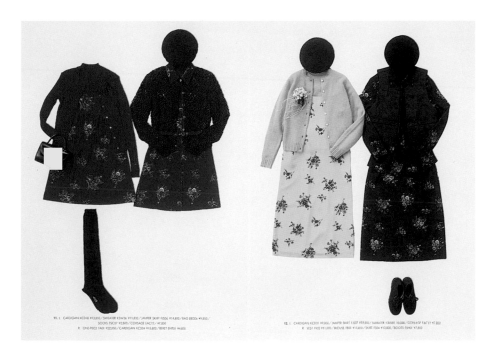

P / X CO., LTD. •

㈱ピー・エックス

Apparel maker / アパレル メーカー
Product catalogue / 製品案内
1995
size: 297×210 mm

Fashion • 039

• **FUSEN USAGI CORPORATION**

フーセンウサギ㈱

Apparel maker / アパレル メーカー
Product catalogue / 製品案内
1995
CD: Paul Smith
AD: Alan Aboud
P: Sandro Sodano
size: 225×225 mm

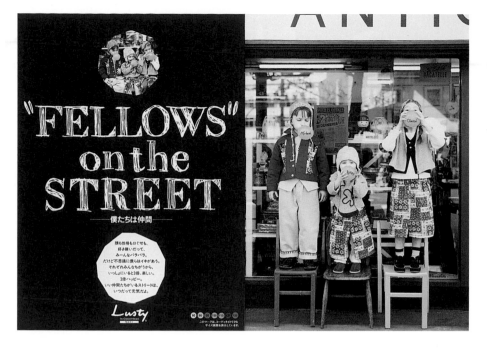

FUSEN USAGI CORPORATION •

フーセンウサギ㈱

Apparel maker / アパレル メーカー

Product catalogue / 製品案内

1995

CD: Shuji Horiguchi　堀口秀司

AD: Masaru Iba　伊庭　勝

D: Yumiko Fujimoto　藤本 由美子

P: Shizuo Takayama　高山静男

CW: Motoko Hayashi　林 元子

size: 257×183 mm

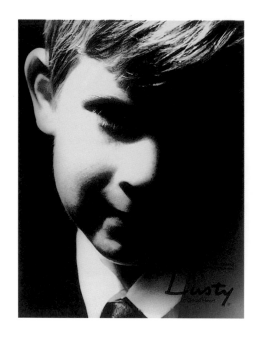

• **FUSEN USAGI CORPORATION**
フーセンウサギ㈱

Apparel maker / アパレル メーカー
Product catalogue / 製品案内
1993
AD, D: Yoshimaru Takahashi　高橋善丸
D: Hitoshi Tomiyasu　富安　均
P: Yasunori Tamamoto　玉本恵則
size: 320×245 mm

FUSEN USAGI CORPORATION •

フーセンウサギ㈱

Apparel maker / アパレル メーカー

Product catalogue / 製品案内

1993

AD, D: Yoshimaru Takahashi　高橋善丸

D: Hitoshi Tomiyasu　富安　均

P: Yasunori Tamamoto　玉本恵則

size: 320×245 mm

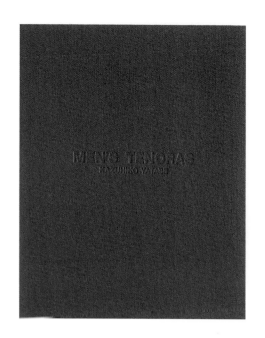

- **TENORAS CO., LTD.**
  ㈱ティノラス

  Apparel maker / アパレル メーカー
  Product catalogue / 製品案内
  1989
  AD: Kyoji Kawai　河合恭誌
  D: Sojiro Saito　斎藤 壮司朗
  P: Kaoru Ijima　伊島 薫
  size: 152×116 mm

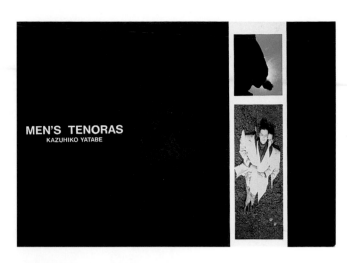

TENORAS CO., LTD. •

㈱ティノラス

Apparel maker / アパレル メーカー
Product catalogue / 製品案内
1990
AD: Kyoji Kawai　河合恭誌
D: Sojiro Saito　斎藤 壮司朗
P: Kaoru Ijima　伊島 薫
size: 155×217 mm

Fashion • 045

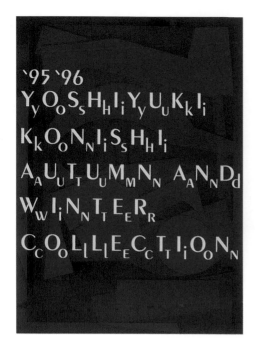

'95 '96
YyOoSsHhIiYyUuKkIi
KkOoNnIiSsHhIi
AAUuTUuMMNn AANnDd
WwIiNnTtEeRr
CcOoLlLlEeCcTtIiOoNn

• **FICCE UOMO**

㈱フィッチェ ウォーモ

Apparel maker / アパレル メーカー
Product catalogue / 製品案内
1995
CD: Jin Hidaka　飛鷹　仁
AD: Takayoshi Tsuchiya　土屋孝元
size: 364×260 mm

FICCE UOMO •

㈱フィッチェ ウォーモ

Apparel maker / アパレル メーカー
Product catalogue / 製品案内
1994
CD: Jin Hidaka 飛鷹　仁
AD: Takayoshi Tsuchiya 土屋孝元
size: 364×260 mm

Fashion • 047

• **P / X CO., LTD.**

㈱ピー・エックス

Apparel maker / アパレル メーカー
Product catalogue / 製品案内
1995
size: 297×210 mm

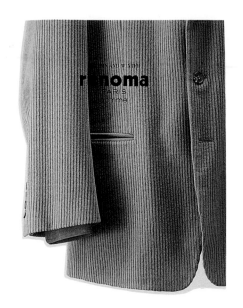

LANEROSSI & •
ALPHACUBIC CO., LTD.

ラネロッシ & アルファキュービック㈱

Apparel maker / アパレル メーカー

Product catalogue / 製品案内

1994

AD: Noriyasu Hoshina　保科憲保

D: Okumiya Design Office

奥宮デザイン室

size: 800×520 mm

Fashion • 049

The main theme for this Fall is
"A fresh emanation of TRAD".
Using enamel and intaglio, we will show you
the 1994 FIN version of "Traditional Style".
Not only that...
We will show you all of our Elegant, Sporty,
Club, and Punk styles which will be
fashionably coordinate for you.

943-1006 Color:Black,Brown,Red,Navy,Beige / 15,800YEN July / End

943-1019 Color:Black,Brown,Pink,Green,Navy,Beige / 14,800YEN July / End

943-1001 Color:Black,Brown,Beige,Gray,Black Smooth / 15,800YEN July / Early

943-1226 Color:Black,Brown,Beige,Wine,Black Check,Red Check,Green Check,Gray Check / 9,800YEN July / End

943-170
Color:Ivory,Black,Navy,Beige,Light Blue,Red Check
5,900YEN July / Early

943-1005
Color:Black,Red,Green,Gray
9,800YEN July / Middle

Come on...open your eyes.
When you change the way of life,
you also change the way you dress.
My personal style varies, and now,
I'm a punk.
One day though... You'll see...

943-1437 Color:Black,Brown / 16,800YEN August / Early

943-1432 Color:Black,Brown,Beige,Camel / 13,800YEN July / End

943-1431 Color:Black,Brown,Beige,Camel / 13,800YEN July / End

- **FIN INC.**

㈱フィン

Shoe manufacturer / シューズ メーカー
Product catalogue / 製品案内
1994
CD, AD: Jinshi Imagawa　今川仁志
D: Yoshiko Uchida　内田良子
P: Hiroki Endo　遠藤宏樹
CW: Keiko Sakamoto　坂本圭子
DF: KONG STUDIO CO., LTD.
㈱コング・スタジオ
size: 257×182 mm

WANNA
BE
LIKE
L OLITA

ALWAYS BE A
LITTLE GIRL
PRETTY
CUTE AND SWEET.

SMILE AT ME WITH
OPEN CHARM

Be my friend with that wide generous
smile and then take my hand.
Together we'll play games that kids play
and eat our cookies side by side.
Don't run from me and play hide and seek,
always be with me and smile.

FIN INC.

Funny when she wants to be and a
little sexy when she's clever.
Forever a mischievous child by nature.

H EALTHY
&
S EXY

LIKE THE IDEA SIMPLE
IS BEST, NATURAL
IS BEAUTIFUL.
THE LEAST AMOUNT OF
WORRY GIVES
THE BEST RESULTS.

I want to be in tune with nature, to
feel like a cloudless blue sky that
stretches her arms wide in a sexy embrace.
I throw my clothes on with a casual
elegance to create an image harmonious
with spring's rebirds.
I'm refreshed.

Polished

Unstudied

Sandals will be popular big this year!
Our next line up will be an SANDALS.
Till next time.

The most versatile high-summer
footwear is the simple sandals
— easy elegance —

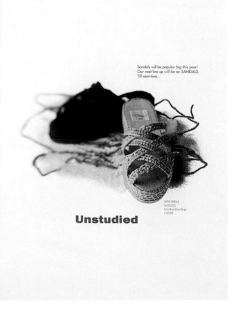

FIN INC. •

㈱フィン

Shoe manufacturer / シューズ メーカー
Product catalogue / 製品案内
1994
CD, AD: Jinshi Imagawa　今川仁志
D: Yoshiko Uchida　内田良子
P: Hiroki Endo　遠藤宏樹
CW: Keiko Sakamoto　坂本圭子
DF: KONG STUDIO CO., LTD.

㈱コング・スタジオ

size: 297×210 mm

Accessories • 051

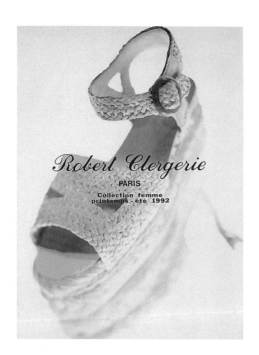

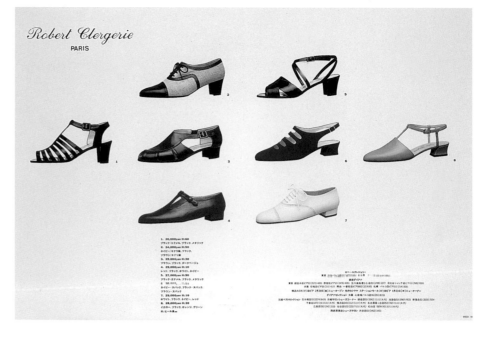

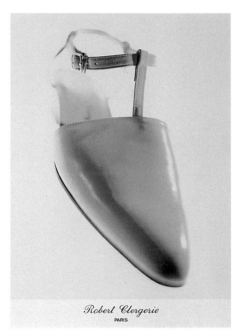

• **DIANA CO., LTD.**

ダイアナ㈱

Shoe manufacturer / シューズ メーカー
Product catalogue / 製品案内
1992
AD: Kyoji Kawai　河合恭誌
D: Kenji Harada　原田健次
P: Kenji Toma　藤間謙二
size: 297×210 mm

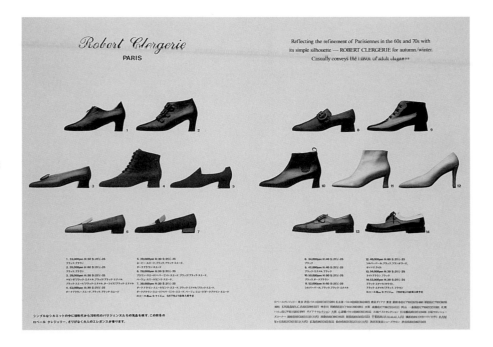

Robert Clergerie
PARIS

Reflecting the refinement of Parisiennes in the 60s and 70s with
its simple silhouette — ROBERT CLERGERIE for autumn/winter.
Casually conveys the flavor of adult elegance.

Robert Clergerie
PARIS
Collection femme automne
hiver 1991-1992

Robert Clergerie
PARIS

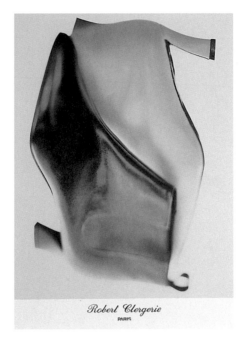

Robert Clergerie
PARIS

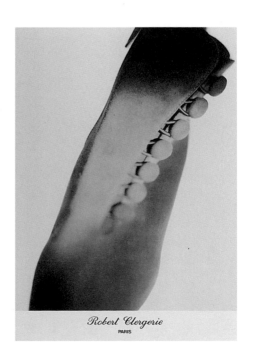

Robert Clergerie
PARIS

Robert Clergerie
PARIS

DIANA CO., LTD. •

ダイアナ㈱

Shoe manufacturer / シューズ メーカー

Product catalogue / 製品案内

1991

AD: Kyoji Kawai　河合恭誌

D: Kenji Harada　原田健次

P: Kenji Toma　藤間謙二

size: 307×215 mm

Accessories • 053

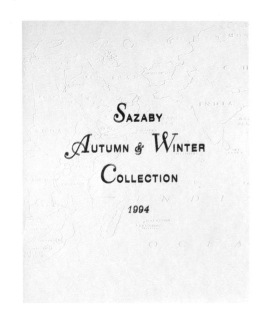

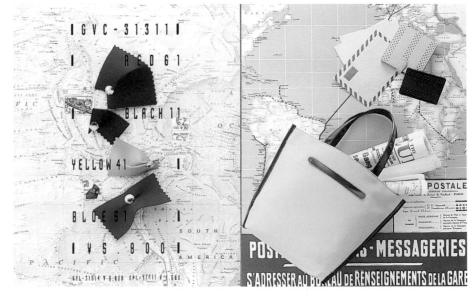

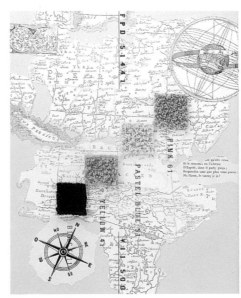

- **SAZABY INC.**

㈱サザビー

Home accessories supplier /
家具・アクセサリー・雑貨等輸入製造販売
Product catalogue / 製品案内
1994
AD, DF: Sazaby Graphic Design
サザビー グラフィックデザイン
D: Hatsuko Kobayashi /
Chie Kusakari　小林初子 / 草刈千絵
P: Bokuyo Tarao / Arte-Estudio La Blar
多羅尾 牧洋 / ㈱ラ ブラール
size: 187×148 mm

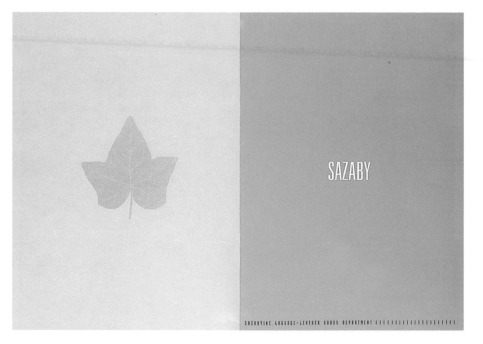

SAZABY

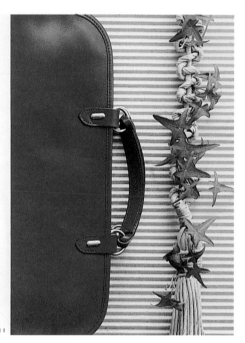

SAZABY INC. •

㈱サザビー

Home accessories supplier /

家具・アクセサリー・雑貨等輸入製造販売

Product catalogue / 製品案内

1994

AD, DF: Sazaby Graphic Design

サザビー グラフィックデザイン

D: Hatsuko Kobayashi /

Chie Kusakari　小林初子 / 草刈千絵

P: Bokuyo Tarao / Arte-Estudio La Blar

多羅尾 牧洋 / ㈱ラ ブラール

size: 210×148 mm

Accessories • 055

JEWELRY BOOK

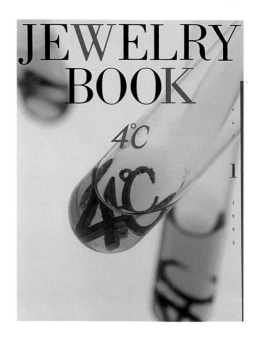

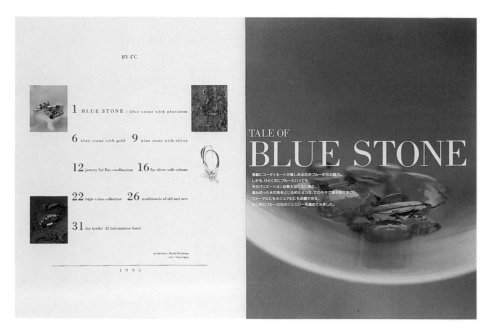

art direction : Miyuki Hirashima
text : Tetsuro Igami

1995

TALE OF BLUE STONE

荒涼にコーディネートが楽しめるのかブルーの石の魅力。
しかも、ひとくちにブルーといっても、
そのバリエーションは数えられないほど。
澄み切った水の色をとじ込めたような、さわやかで清涼感があり
フォーマルにもカジュアルにも活躍できる。
今人気のブルーの石のジュエリーを集めてみました。

BLUE STONE WITH PLATINUM

Photographed by Tetsuya Miura

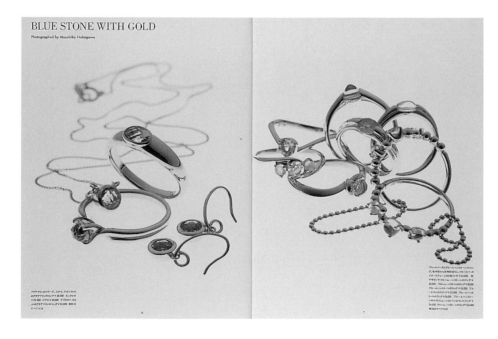

BLUE STONE WITH GOLD

Photographed by Masahiko Nukagawa

• **F.D.C. PRODUCTS CO., LTD.**

㈱エフ・ディ・シィ プロダクツ

Fashion accessories, apparel maker /

アクセサリー・アパレル メーカー

Product catalogue / 製品案内

1995

AD, D: Miyuki Hirashima　平島みゆき

size: 280×215 mm

Photographed by Meisa Fujishiro

hair & make-up · Noriharu Hoshi model · Emma

jewery for fine cordination

コーディネートの魅力は、
何といってもその楽しさでしょう。
見事に決まったコーディネートは、
さりげなく行き届いた好印象を与えます。
コーディネート・ジュエリーのポイントは、
やはり統一感。
バランス良く、すっきりとシンプルに、
品良くまとめました。

12

13

18

19

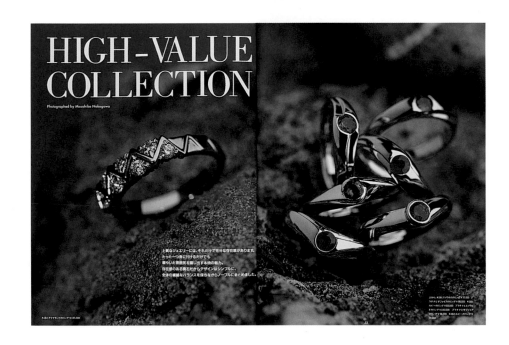

HIGH-VALUE COLLECTION

Photographed by Masahiko Nakagawa

上質なジュエリーには、それだけで十分な存在感があります。
たった一つ身に付けるだけでも
際立いた華麗感を醸し出す本物の魅力。
存在感のある質だからデザインはシンプルに、
全体の繊細なバランスを保ちながらノーブルにまとめました。

22

23

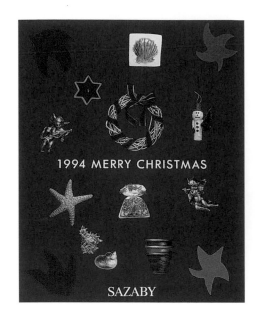

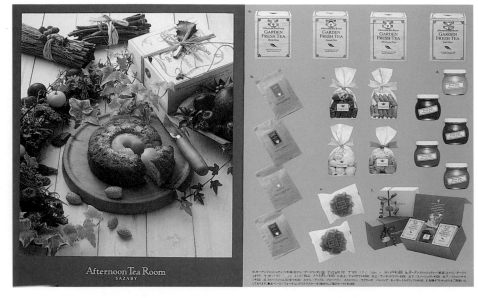

• **SAZABY INC.**

㈱サザビー

Home accessories supplier /

家具・アクセサリー・雑貨等輸入製造販売

Product catalogue / 製品案内

1994

AD, DF: Sazaby Graphic Design

サザビー グラフィックデザイン

D: Hatsuko Kobayashi　小林初子

P: Toshiro Takayama　高山俊郎

size: 240×182 mm

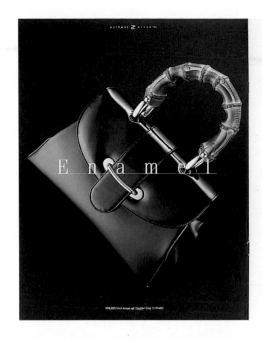

SANKI SHOJI CO., LTD. •

三喜商事㈱

Apparel distributor /

アパレル ディストリビューター

Product catalogue / 製品案内

1995

CD, AD: Yasuyuki Kadokawa　門川泰之

D: Kayoko Yamamoto　山本 香代子

P: Shoichi Kondo　近藤正一

size: 297×220 mm

Accessories • 059

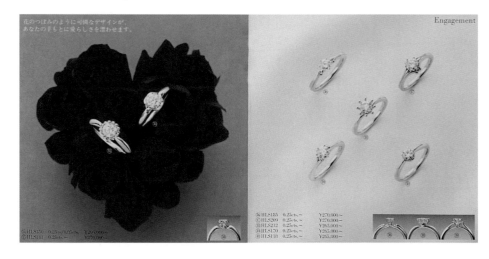

• **ORIENTAL DIAMOND INC.**

㈱オリエンタル ダイヤモンド

Jewelry manufacturer /

ジュエリー メーカー

Product catalogue / 製品案内

1995

CD: Naoko Harada　原田尚子

AD: Shunji Yoshioka　吉岡俊司

D: Mayumi Arakawa　荒川真弓

P: Kenichi Higashi　東　健一

I: Goro Sasaki　佐々木 悟郎

CW: Yasuyuki Morishita　森下康幸

size: 120×120 mm

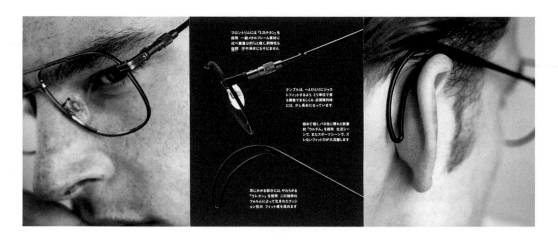

カラダ、動く。メガネ、動かない。

MARUMAN OPTICAL CO., LTD. •

マルマン オプティカル㈱

Eye-wear manufacturer /

メガネ メーカー

Product catalogue / 製品案内

1993

CD: Junzi Hara　原 純志

AD, D: Masaru Iwata　岩田 優

P: Ryo Kazami　香水 亮

CW: Yasunari Taniguchi　谷口泰成

DF: Base Ad Creates Co., Ltd.

㈱ベイス・アド・クリエイツ

size: 170×135 mm

Accessories • 061

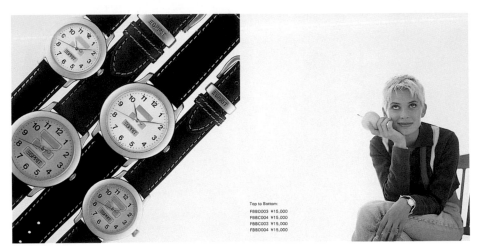

• **SEIKO CORPORATION**

㈱服部セイコー

Watch and clock marketer /

時計等販売

Product catalogue / 製品案内

1994

CD: Roberto Carra

AD: Leslie Kushner

P: Victoria Pearson / Karen Steffens

DF: Esprit International Design Studio,

San Francisco

size: 150×150 mm

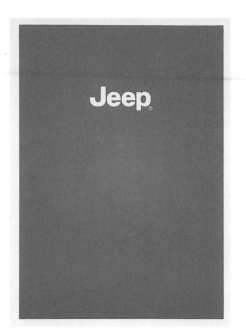

ナチュラルな自分へと還る時間。
4WDの代名詞とも言うべき名車、ジープ。
その名を耳にするとき、僕たちはなぜか懐かしさとともに愛着を感じる。
1941年アメリカで生まれたジープは、半世紀ものあいだ、
オフロードを走破するタフなクルマとして、
世界中の人々に愛され、今も人々を魅了し続けている。
ソフィスティケートされた「チェロキー」と、
ジープ本来のヘビーデューティーさを持つ「ラングラー」。
今、ジープのコンセプトを受け継いで生まれたリストウォッチ、誕生。
乾いたアスファルト、草原のざわめき、大地の匂い、水面の静寂・・・ジープ。
それは、アウトドアマインドをいつも忘れない人の腕にふさわしい。

COMPASS

きみは今、何処にいるのだろう。

何処から来て、
今、何処にいて、
これから
何処へ行こうとしているのか。
時々見失いそうになる行く先を
取り戻す時、新たな冒険への入口が
そこに、待っている。

7-JP2003-31 ¥21,000
8-JP2003-61 ¥21,000
9-JP2003-01 ¥21,000

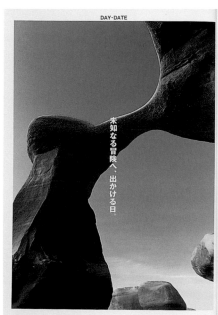

DAY·DATE

未知なる冒険へ、出かける日。

小さなダイヤルの中に
表示される日付・曜日・24時間計。
今日までのことを思い出し
明日からはじまる新しい出来事に思いを馳せながら
胸おどる満天の星空の下
シュラフにくるまった。

13-JP2005-61 ¥19,000
14-JP2005-31 ¥19,000
15-JP2005-01 ¥19,000

J.OSAWA & CO., LTD. •

㈱大沢商会

Trading company / 商社

1994

AD: Keisuke Kimura 木村経典

D: Takeshi Tezuka 手塚 毅

P: Naohiro Ichiki 一色直裕

CW: Hiroshi Yamazaki 山崎博志

size: 182×128 mm

Accessories • 063

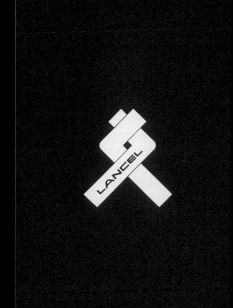

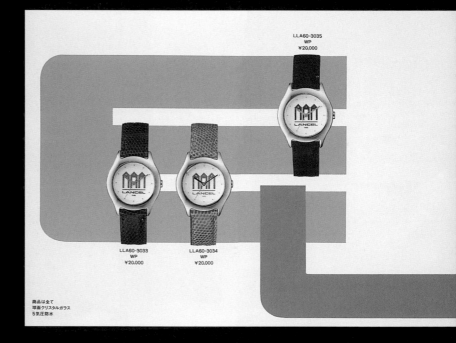

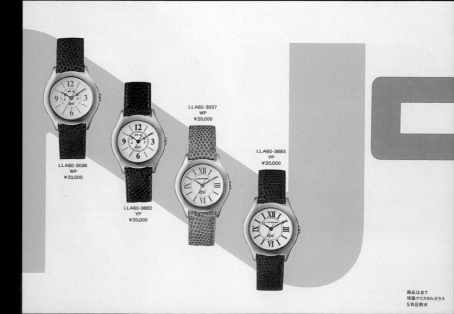

- **CITIZEN TRADING CO., LTD**

  シチズン商事㈱

  Watch manufacturer / 時計等販売

  Product catalogue / 製品案内

  1995

  AD: Hideaki Muto　武藤秀明

  D: Chikako Ogawa　小川 千賀子

  P: Shoichi Kondo　近藤正一

  CW: Shingo Takeuchi　竹内慎吾

  DF: Muto Office　武藤事務所

  size: 158×110 mm

ALPHA CUBIC

CITIZEN TRADING CO., LTD.

シチズン商事㈱

Watch manufacturer / 時計等販売

Product catalogue / 製品案内

1995

AD: Hideaki Muto　武藤秀明

D: Chikako Ogawa　小川 千賀子

P: Shoichi Kondo　近藤正一

DF: Muto Office　武藤事務所

size: 160×160 mm

EXCEED COLLECTION

CITIZEN

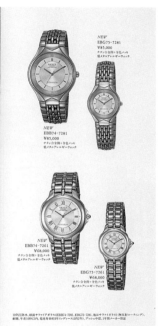

• **CITIZEN TRADING CO., LTD.**

シチズン商事㈱

Watch manufacturer / 時計等販売

Product catalogue / 製品案内

1995

CD: Masakazu Matsuba　松葉雅一

AD, D: Hiroshi Nishio　西尾　浩

P: Keigo Ohira　大平啓吾

CW: Kimiaki Cho　張　公明

DF: J2 Complex Inc.

㈱ジェイ・コンプレックス

PD: Jun Nakamura　中村　潤

size: 222×110 mm

CITIZEN TRADING CO., LTD. •

シチズン商事㈱

Watch manufacturer / 時計等販売

Product catalogue / 製品案内

1995

CD, CW: Tatsuro Takahashi　高橋達郎

AD, D, CW: Takeshi Shinmichi

新道武司

DF: Takahashi Room Co., Ltd.

㈱高橋ルーム

PD: Kiyoshi Okamoto　岡本　清

size: 175×175 mm

CLINICAL BEAUTY

BODY MIND LIFE

〔アイ脱毛〕
弱い電流と高周波で
毛乳頭と呼ばれる皮下組織を自然退化させる
硬毛から軟毛まで処理が早い

〔D只脱毛〕
うぶ毛や軟毛に、少しだけ気になるムダ毛を
ピックアップして脱毛することも

〔ハニー〕
脱ヤニとハチミツをあわせた
ワックスタイプの脱毛システム
老化角質も取り除いて、ツルツルの肌肌に

〔ブリーチ〕
わずか3分で、スピーディに脱色
個人の肌色や毛質にあわせて、自然な仕上りに

〔ムース〕
保湿効果でやさしいたわりながら
すみやかに脱毛。敏感な肌や乾燥した肌に

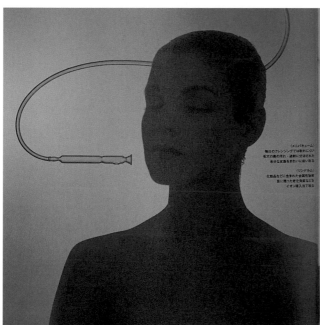

〔メニキュアーム〕
毎日のクレンジングでは取れにくい
毛穴の奥の汚れ・過剰に分泌される
余分な皮脂をきれいに洗い取る

〔リジデルム〕
化粧品などに含まれた各種加湿
肌に残った皮脂残留などを
イオン導入法で取る

〔GXパック〕
24種類のハーブエキスを
分量で素材を加減して、一人ひとり異なったパックを
エステティシャンがその場の肌質に合わせて調合

〔MSシステム〕
赤、黒、青の先生肌のトラブルに
合わせて使い分け。オゾンとマイクロマッサージの
相乗効果で各種トラブルを解消

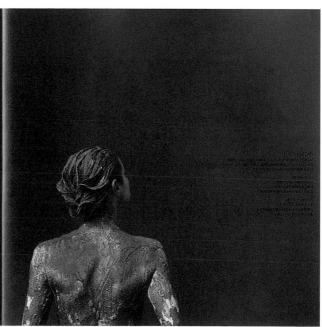

〔パルス・ウェーブ〕
低周波を使った筋肉トレーニング
やせたい部分をひきしめる

〔バイオトーン〕
マシーンによるマッサージ
やさしい振動で凝った筋肉や脂肪をもみほぐす

CLEANSING

洗顔──それは1日に2度に欠かせない素肌への慈愛でもある。
朝、眠っている間にかいた汗をきれいに洗い流したい。
気分を引きしめるモーニング・クレンジング。
夜、メイクを落とし、肌に残る汗やけがれを清潔にするイブニング・クレンジング。
1日2度の洗浄が、あなたのスキンケアの基本となる。

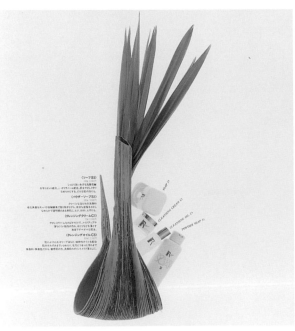

《ソープ S3》
¥50 3,000円
とろりとした泡立ち。しっとりと洗い上げる洗顔石鹸

《パウダー・ソープ S1》
¥50 2,500円
余分な角質をやさしく取り除きます。きめを整える洗顔料。

《クレンジング・クリーム C1》
¥50 4,000円
やさしいクリームのなめらかさで、メイクアップや
落ちにくい汚れを浮かす。ほつらりとした美肌

《クレンジング・オイル C5》
¥60 3,500円
汚れにくいオイルタイプで、植物性オイル配合。しっとり洗い上げます。
無香料・無着色だから、植物性の洗顔料にもやさしいメイク落とし。

MASK PACK

せっかくクレンジングをして、素肌が爽快をしても。
そのあとのケアがなくては、美しさは一瞬時のものとなってしまう。
ムズずしい素肌を乾かさないうちに、キープすることを忘れてほしくない。リッシュさの持続でもある。
肌にやさしい高品質コラーゲンと天然成分が、あなたの素肌を生まれたままの肌状に。

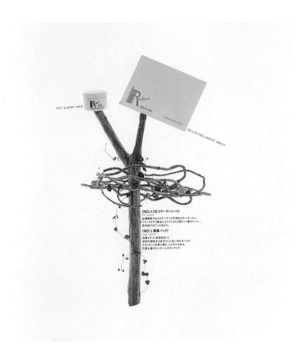

《NO.4-15 コラーゲン シート》
¥60 1,800円
成分解剖でもエステージで可愛化コラーゲンでも
フリーズドライ製法によりうまれたら潤うる素肌のマスク。
新生素やけるけに肌のもの。

《NO.5 海藻 パック》
¥60 2,500円
海藻よりの天然成分配合
潤いを与えるお肌を潤す。しっとりなめらか肌へ。
花嫁を通ぬしいオールスキンタイプ。

SKIN CARE

肌は水分である。季節や現実の移ろいに応じて。
素肌の状態は変化してくれる。肌は若い一肌と同じ変化をするもあろうとのだ。
バルランスこそ、微妙なるくらべをケアするのでおいてもいくのだろうトレム。
あいかわらずや決する汚れを落とす、クレンジングとクレームの中の
ラインアップが、あなたの輝きを深めてくれる。

《ミルクローズ S17》
¥56 3,500円
肌を潤し、やわらかな洗顔料
肌にもつ、素キンの自然と水分と潤いのとなる洗顔料。

《シェービングパウダー S6》
¥56 3,000円
アプリ汚れのなすフィルンけの洗顔料です。
私の汚れにより、汗をシェービングパウダーでしめ気持ちよ。
きめを整えて。

《フェイシャル・ソープ S19》
¥58 2,000円
石鹸ならでの持続を感じ
肌に潤いのリッチの泡をと。
しっとり、クリーミーな肌残し。

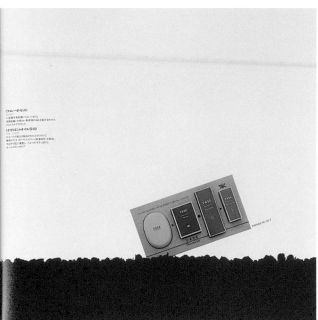

MAKE UP

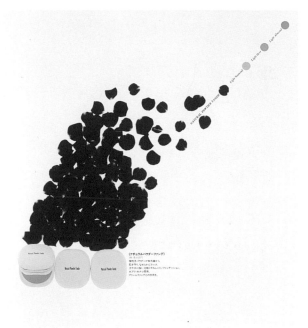

P 068 ～ 071

TOKYO BEAUTY CENTER •

東京ビューティーセンター

Beauty salon / エステティック サロン

Product catalogue / 製品案内

1989

CD, AD, D: Atsushi Ebina　海老名 淳

P: Yoshikazu Hagiwara / Shoji Sato

萩原佳一 / 佐藤正治

CW: Takao Fujino　藤野孝夫

size: 255×260 mm

Cosmetics • 071

DELICATI TRATTAMENTI DI PULIZIA

L'ORÉAL
PROFUMERIA

Plénitude

Per pelli secche e sensibili, la linea *Massima Tolleranza*

Il 60% delle donne dichiara di avere la pelle sensibile, una pelle cioè reattiva. Spesso si parla di pelli sottili e secche che non reagiscono bene alle variazioni della temperatura, allo stress e all'inquinamento. Queste pelli fragili hanno esigenze specifiche: la garanzia dell'innocuità al prodotto e la certezza di una pulizia perfetta ma allo stesso tempo dolce e delicata.

Il Latte Detergente Vellutato rispetta le pelli secche e sensibili

Questa formula risponde con efficacia ad una doppia aspettativa: eliminare con dolcezza le tracce del trucco e di latte le impurità e apportare un effetto idratante immediato.
Il Latte Detergente Vellutato sfrutta un'innovazione tecnologica che si basa dell'associazione di due materie prime:
un nuovo estere/olio dolce detergente.
Quest'olio concentrato al 30% nella formula è selezionato per i Laboratori de L'Oréal offre:
• un migliore potere detergente;
• non è grasso al latto
• grazie alle sue proprietà emollienti rende l'applicazione particolarmente piacevole
• una massima tolleranza: delicatissimo per pelli sensibili
un copolimero
Questo copolimero modifica la texture classica dell'emulsione permettendole di rimanere leggera e di essere assorbita immediatamente dalla pelle donando una sensazione di freschezza. Inoltre accresce il potere detergente dell'olio che permette di lasciare la pelle pulita e non grassa.

Il Tonico Addolcente Idratante risveglia il colorito in dolcezza

Complemento al Latte Detergente Vellutato, questo tonico apporta un tocco finale in tutta dolcezza alla pulizia delle pelli secche e sensibili.
Il Tonico Addolcente Idratante risveglia il colorito.
La sua formula senz'alcool è stata arricchita con un agente addolcente idratante. Per poter rivendicare la loro totale tollerabilità, queste formule sono state oggetto, nell'arco di diverse settimane, di test specifici sperimentati sotto controllo dermatologico su pelli particolarmente intolleranti e sensibili.

6

Pelli secche e sensibili:
obiettivo dolcezza con Plénitude.
Il gesto vellutato di un
latte vellutante.
La freschezza della rosa per un
tonico delicato e dolce.

Plénitude

Pelli miste o tendenti al grasso

Quattro donne su 10 dichiarano di avere una pelle mista o tendente al grasso.
Le loro preferenze sono rivolte a purificare e apportare freschezza alla pelle.
Per queste ragioni sono grandi consumatrici del tonico.

Il Tonico Rinfrescante Purificante rivitalizza e tonifica

Libera la pelle dalle sue impurità, elimina l'eccesso di sebo rispettando l'equilibrio dell'epidermide.
Specificamente concepito per le pelli miste o tendenti al grasso, questa formula associa:
• un agente specifico che purifica e rinfresca la pelle
• un composto astringente all'estratto di biancospino per restringere i pori della pelle e tonificarla.

8

Pelli miste o tendenti al grasso:
obiettivo purezza Plénitude.
Il gesto purificante di un tonico
rinfrescante.

Plénitude

Per tutti i tipi di pelle

Il trattamento per la pulizia di tutti i tipi di pelle di Plénitude si basa su 3 azioni:
• eliminare perfettamente qualsiasi traccia di impurità, di trucco e di cellule morte
• rispettare la pelle, cioè detergere senza aggredire
• equilibrare il tasso d'idratazione dell'epidermide per mantenere la freschezza e la tonicità.

Il Latte Detergente Addolcente

Elimina con dolcezza le impurità e le tracce di trucco.
La sua formula, arricchita con la lipoproteine, è indicata per tutti i tipi di pelle e lascia l'epidermide pulita, fresca, morbida e idratata.

Il Tonico Addolcente

È il complemento ideale del Latte Detergente.
Purifica e rinfresca la pelle.
La sua formula senz'alcool alla pro-vitamina B5 tonifica e ammorbidisce con dolcezza l'epidermide.

10

Per tutti i tipi di pelle:
un latte e un tonico per una
perfetta pulizia, nel rispetto totale
della pelle del viso.

• **L'ORÉAL**

Cosmetics manufacturer / 化粧品メーカー

Product catalogue / 製品案内

1994

CD, D: Giorgio Rocco

P: Images Photography

CW: Anna Andreuzzi

DF: Giorgio Rocco Communications
Design Consultants

size: 297×210 mm

Il colore che rende più belle... con semplicità

Casting è uno shampoo color completamente nuovo.
Casting realizza l'alleanza della dolcezza
e della tenacità al servizio di un colore molto naturale
ed estremamente brillante.

CASTING

L'ORÉAL
PROFUMERIE

I prodotti di colorazione sul mercato

Oggi esistono due grandi tipi di prodotti di colorazione
sul mercato:

La colorazione permanente
che esercita due azioni simultanee:
la decolorazione e la ripigmentazione dei capelli, grazie
all'azione combinata di un agente ossidante (il più efficace
è l'acqua ossigenata) e di una soluzione alcalina
(spesso l'ammoniaca)

La colorazione semi-permanente
che agisce solo sullo strato esterno del capello.
La sua formulazione non contiene né acqua ossigenata,
né ammoniaca, ma di conseguenza la sua azione
è più blanda e non dura che lo spazio di qualche shampoo.

Casting
un nuovo tipo di colorazione:
la colorazione tono su tono

Casting non trasforma il colore di partenza dei capelli,
ma lo arricchisce di nuances naturali nella sua stessa tonalità.
Questa è la colorazione tono su tono.

**Casting
è senza ammoniaca**

La sua originalità risulta da un perfetto equilibrio dei suoi
componenti. Utilizza infatti un agente alcalino infinitamente più
dolce dell'ammoniaca, dosato in modo da ottenere la formazione
di pigmenti colorati, senza gonfiare eccessivamente la fibra,
ed è associato ad un polimero cosmetico brevettato da L'Oréal.
È il metodo dolce Casting per una dolcezza incomparabile.

**Casting dona
un risultato durevole**

Insensibile al ritmo frequente degli shampoo il colore ottenuto
rimane brillante e luminoso nel tempo.
Inoltre, grazie all'azione tono su tono, rende particolarmente
discreto il fenomeno della ricrescita.

L'estrema brillantezza di un bello naturale

**Per colori luminosi
e naturali**
Casting rispetta le variazioni della pigmentazione naturale.
Mantiene infatti le sfumature naturali della capigliatura
arricchendola di nuances naturali e di riflessi luminosi.
Casting ridona vita al colore.

**Per un'estrema
brillantezza**
Casting agisce come un vero trattamento cosmetico.
Grazie alla presenza di un polimero cationico che si fissa
sulla fibra capillare (brevetto L'Oreal n.1063.131).
Casting conferisce ai capelli una dolcezza, una morbidezza
e una brillantezza assolutamente incredibili.

**Per coprire
i capelli bianchi**
Casting è il prodotto ideale per mascherare i primi capelli
bianchi (fino al 60%).
Colorati in trasparenza si mischiano e si confondono
con il resto della capigliatura.
Più la percentuale dei capelli bianchi è importante,
più si riflesso sarà marcato per donare ancora più rilievo
e luminosità all'acconciatura.

**Per una colorazione
naturale e duratura**
Casting è inoltre perfetto per chi desidera non cambiare
in modo definitivo il suo colore naturale e considera
le colorazioni semi-permanenti una soluzione provvisoria.

L'OREAL •

Cosmetics manufacturer / 化粧品メーカー

Product catalogue / 製品案内

1993

CD, D: Giorgio Rocco

P: Archives L'Oréal

CW: Anna Andreuzzi

DF: Giorgio Rocco Communications

Design Consultants

size: 297×210 mm

• SHISEIDO CO., LTD.

㈱資生堂

Cosmetics manufacturer / 化粧品メーカー

Product catalogue / 製品案内

1994

CD: Toshio Yamagata　山形季央

AD, D: Adlai Stock

P: Scott Morgan

CW: Douglas Toews

DF: Shiseido Co., Ltd. International

Marketing Dep. Creative Group

㈱資生堂 国際マーケティング部

クリエイティブ・グループ

size: 210×148 mm

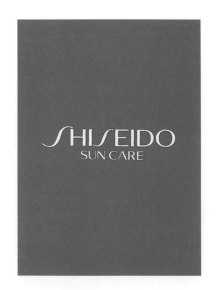

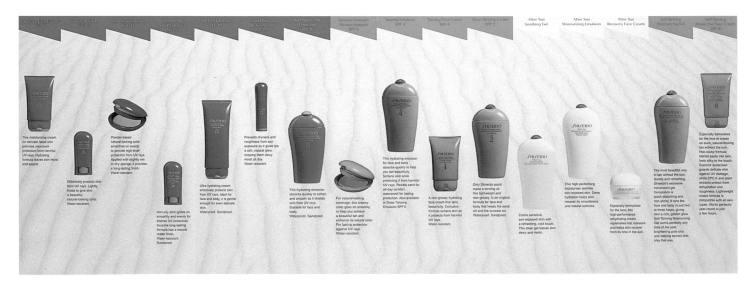

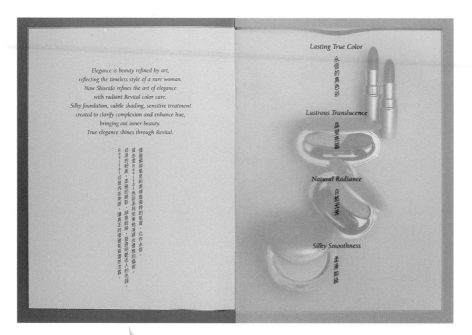

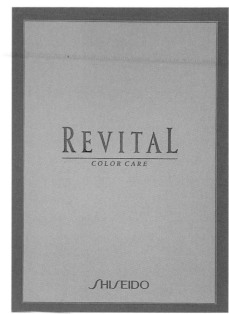

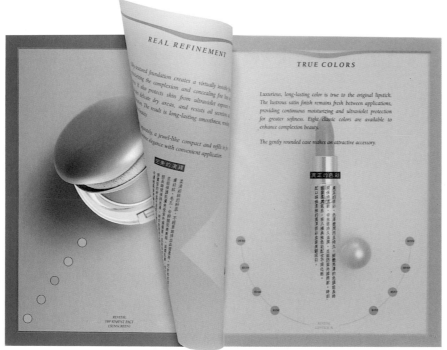

SHISEIDO CO., LTD. •

㈱資生堂

Cosmetics manufacturer / 化粧品メーカー

Product catalogue / 製品案内

1994

AD, D: Adlai Stock

P: Seiichi Nakamura 中村成一

CW: Ann Colville

DF: Shiseido Co., Ltd. International

Marketing Dep. Creative Group

㈱資生堂 国際マーケティング部

クリエイティブ・グループ

size: 210×148 mm

Cosmetics • 075

幸せに輝く香り、トレゾア。

その、ひとしずくは、
愛するひとと過ごすときのような、
ときめき、しあわせ─。
のびやかで存在感にあふれ、
人生を美しく演じる香り。
1935年、香水のブランドとして生まれた
ランコムが、現代を楽しむ、
しなやかな女性に捧げます。
女優イザベラ・ロッセリーニを映す、
華やかで気品ある香水。
情熱によって生きるひとへ。
幸せに輝く香り、トレゾア。

神秘のエッセンスに香りたつ、バラの調べ。

白バラ、鈴蘭、ライラック…麗しい花々の香りに、みずみずしい果実が溶け
あいます。ピーチとアプリコットが奏でる、フルーティなかろやかさ。そして、アイ
リスとヘリオトープによって、いちだんときわだつ、バラの香り。トップノートの
知性とミドルノートの感性が調和して生まれる、微妙なニュアンス。さらに、基
調となるアンバー、びゃくだん、ムスクが、官能的な世界へと誘います。深い
魅力を秘めた、フローラル セミオリエンタル。永遠に抱きしめていたい香り。

PARFUM
トレゾァ パルファン　トレゾァ パルファン スプレー

EAU DE PARFUM
トレゾァ オー ドゥ パルファン　トレゾァ オー ドゥ パルファン スプレー

• **COSMELOR LTD.**
  LANCÔME DIVISION
  ㈱コスメロール ランコム ディヴィジョン

  Cosmetics manufacturer / 化粧品メーカー
  Product catalogue / 製品案内
  1991
  size: 150×150 mm

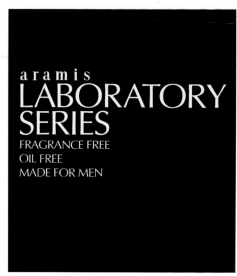

ARAMIS •

アラミス

Cosmetics manufacturer / 化粧品メーカー

Product catalogue / 製品案内

1994, 95

size: 183×163 mm

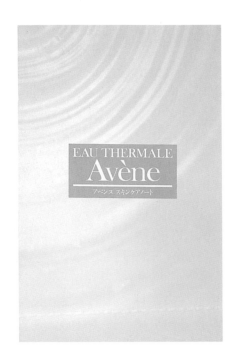

- **PIERRE FABRE JAPON**

㈱ピエール ファーブル ジャポン

Cosmetics importer & distributor /

化粧品輸入販売

Product catalogue / 製品案内

1994

size: 182×115 mm

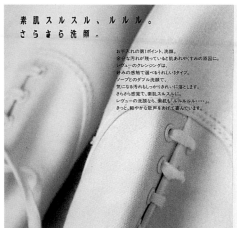

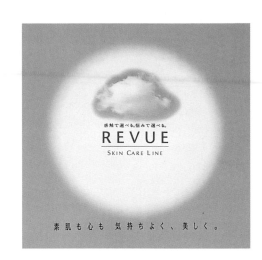

KANEBO, LTD. •
COSMETICS DIVISION

鐘紡㈱ カネボウ化粧品本部

Cosmetics manufacturer / 化粧品メーカー

Product catalogue / 製品案内

1995

A: Japan Marketing Services

ジャパン マーケティング サービス

AD: Tatsuya Kawaminami　川南達也

D: Narumi Mizoi　溝井成美

CW: Miyako Kishi　岸 都

size: 167×167 mm

きれいになる本
k i r e i 1995 Autumn Vol.10

〈拡大特集〉
ふたつの顔を
メイクする

女性であれば誰もが、ふたつの顔をもっている…そう言ったら信じますか？
たとえば眉をナチュラルにするか、細いアーチ型眉にするかだけで、
顔は劇的にふたつになります。色づかいはもちろん、
質感の使い分けでも、顔の印象はがらりと変わるもの。
だからこの秋のテーマは〈自分自身の発見〉。難しいテクニックなしに、
ふたつの顔をメイクし分ける方法を身につければ、
きれいになる可能性は2倍にも3倍にもなるのではないでしょうか。

そこで乾かないマット
テスティモから、マットタイプの口紅登場！

でもマットのカサつきはイヤ……

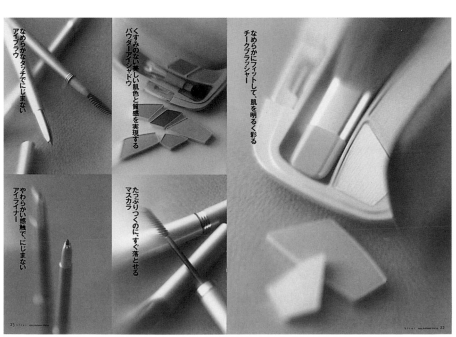

なめらかなタッチでにじまない
アイブラウ

やわらかい感触でにじまない
アイライナー

くすみのない美しい肌色と質感を実現する
パウダーアイシャドウ

たっぷりつくのに、すぐ落とせる
マスカラ

なめらかにフィットして、肌を明るく彩る
チークブラッシャー

• KANEBO, LTD.
COSMETICS DIVISION

鐘紡㈱ カネボウ化粧品本部

Cosmetics manufacturer / 化粧品メーカー

Product catalogue / 製品案内

1995

A, CW: Hakuhodo Incorporated

㈱博報堂

AD: Koji Ono（Diamond Head's）

小野光治（ダイアモンド・ヘッズ）

D: Hideyuki Suzuki（Diamond Head's）

鈴木英之（ダイアモンド・ヘッズ）

P: Shoichi Kondo 近藤正一

I: Michiyo Shirahama 白浜 美千代

S: Keiko Suzuki 鈴木恵子

size: 210×148 mm

〈拡大特集〉私だけのスキンケアをさがす〔特別編〕
もっと正しく、化粧品選び

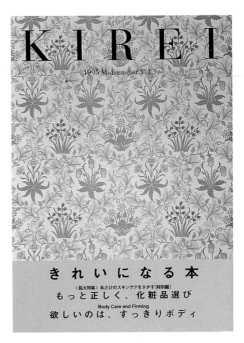

KIREI
1995 Midsummer Vol.9

きれいになる本
〈拡大特集〉私だけのスキンケアをさがす〔特別編〕
もっと正しく、化粧品選び
Body Care and Firming
欲しいのは、すっきりボディ

肌にピタリの3ステップがモノを言う

まずは、洗うこと！

ボディにもある
3つの曲り角

Body Care and Firming

20
30
40

KANEBO, LTD. •
• COSMETICS DIVISION
鐘紡㈱カネボウ化粧品本部

Cosmetics manufacturer / 化粧品メーカー
Product catalogue / 製品案内
1995
A, CW: Hakuhodo Incorporated
㈱博報堂
AD: Koji Ono (Diamond Heads)
小野光治（ダイアモンド・ヘッズ）
D: Hideyuki Suzuki (Diamond Heads)
鈴木英之（ダイアモンド・ヘッズ）
P: Shoichi Kondo 近藤正一
I: Michiyo Shirahama 白浜美千代
S: Keiko Suzuki 鈴木恵子
size: 210×148 mm

Mascara
Accent Stick
BaseColor
EyeColor
LipColor
NailColor
Essence

Maybelline®

NEW

アクティブルック リップスティック L 全5色 各1,500円

blooming my dream

夢が花開く予感。

目を閉じたままでも、耳をふさいでいても
感じてしまうのか、春の足音、競いあうよう
に咲き始めた花たちが、新しい世界に目を
輝かせるように、春は、私たちの世界にも
新鮮なときめきを運んできました。出会い、
旅立ち、チャンス、サクセス、誰にでも
きっとある、人生が美しく開花するとき、
あなたの笑顔がいっそう眩しい瞬間です。

an artist

画家になった初めての作品が
ニューヨーク5番街の画廊に飾られたとき
彼女は29歳。「自分の方法で
言葉にならない自分自身を表現した」
黒い口の強く美しい横顔は
そのままその娘を生きる姿だった。
孤独を愛し、人生を慈しみながらキャンバス
彼女のような生き方をしたいと思う、
自分にしか描けない絵を、
ただひたすらに描くように。

prima donna

その年のシーズンは
カラスにとって特別なものになった。
生まれながらの才能、リリコソプラノ。
豊かな声量にうたわれた
きらめくばかりに美しいその歌声は、
ついにミラノ座を征服したのだから。
苦悩の多い人生に彩りをみせながら、歌劇への
溢れる情熱を花開かせた偉大な歌姫、
魂を感じたいとき、感動に震えたいとき
人は、彼女の歌を聞きたくなる。

- **MAYBELLINE CO., LTD.**

㈱メイベリン

Cosmetics manufacturer / 化粧品メーカー

Product catalogue / 製品案内

1995

CD: Kyoko Tei　梯　京子

P: Yasuto Okumura　奥村康人

CW: Satoko Yamazaki　山崎聡子

size: 182×128 mm

082 • Cosmetics

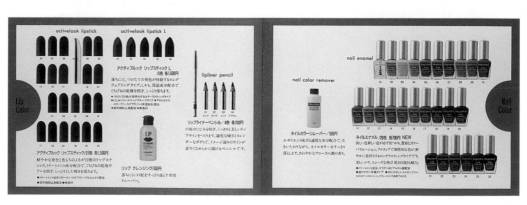

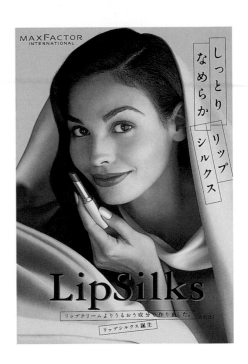

MAX FACTOR INTERNATIONAL
LipSilks

唇がカサついて、口紅がなめらかにすべらない。唇の乾燥が気になるので、下地にリップクリームは欠かせない…。マックス ファクター インターナショナル リップシルクスはそんな女性たちの声にこたえる、新しい口紅。たっぷりとうるおい、唇にはシルクのようななめらかさが生まれる。新処方のモイスト キャッチ システムで、リップクリームよりうるおい、美しい発色とつやが長もち。84年の歴史の中で、世界の女性たちの唇を華やかに彩ってきたマックス ファクター。女性たちのニーズをすばやくキャッチし、つねに高品質な口紅でセンセーショナルを生み出してきました。この秋も、また新しい口紅の誕生です。

モイスト キャッチ システムが、うるおいと、なめらかさを生み出しました。

シルクみたいになめらか。たっぷり、うるおう。リップシルクス新登場。

しっとり　なめらか　リップ　シルクス

リップクリームよりうるおう成分で作りました。(当社比)

リップシルクス誕生

2

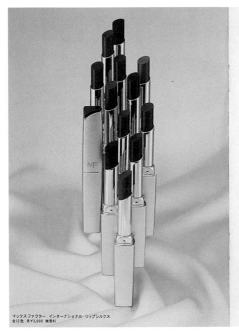

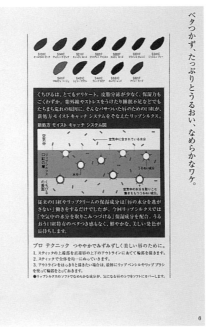

マックス ファクター　インターナショナル リップシルクス
全12色　各¥3,000　無香料

ベタつかず、たっぷりとうるおい、なめらかなワケ。

6

DAILY GLAMOUR
INNOCENT GLAMOUR

11

イノセント グラマー。

40年代アメリカのモダンガールたちの、清潔感あるセクシィなイメージ。唇はナチュラルに、自然の輪郭を生かして仕上げます。目元はすっきりと、色味を感じさせないように仕上げます。ニュートラルでナチュラルなカラーをメインに使います。

MAKE-UP LOOK

[LIP MAKE-UP]

[NAIL MAKE-UP]

[EYE MAKE-UP]

Step (I)

Step (II)

12

**MAX FACTOR •
KABUSHIKI KAISHA**

マックス ファクター㈱

Cosmetics manufacturer / 化粧品メーカー
Product catalogue / 製品案内
1995
size: 182×128 mm

Cosmetics • 083

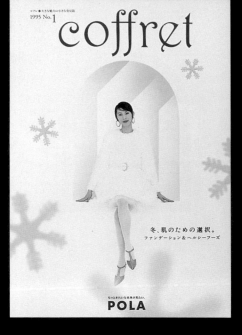

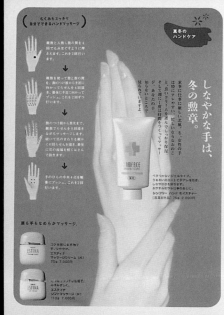

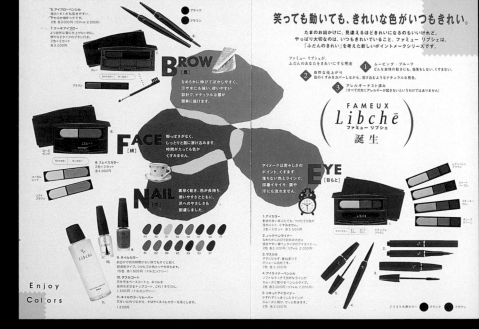

- **POLA COSMETICS INC.**
ポーラ化粧品本舗

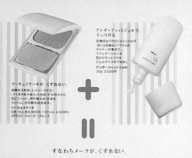

• SENSHUKAI CO., LTD.

㈱千趣会

Mail order retailer / 通信販売

Product catalogue / 製品案内

1993

CD, AD: Koji Kusatsugu　草次耕二

D: Kyoko Izumi　泉　京子

P: Shunji Kaida　海田俊二

CW: Mutsuko Tanaka　田中睦子

DF: Studio VIS Co., Ltd.　㈱スタジオ ビス

size: 148×105 mm

SENSHUKAI CO., LTD. •

㈱千趣会

Mail order retailer / 通信販売

Product catalogue / 製品案内

1994

CD, AD: Koji Kusatsugu　草次耕二

D: Kyoko Izumi　泉　京子

P: Shunji Kaida　海田俊二

CW: Mutsuko Tanaka　田中睦子

DF: Studio VIS Co., Ltd.　㈱スタジオ ビス

size: 270×210 mm

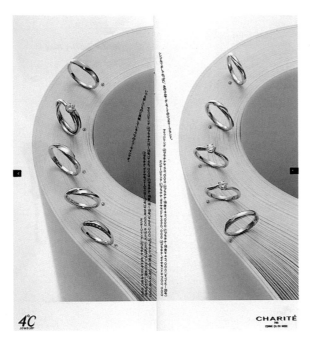

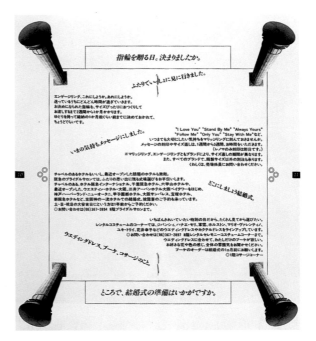

• **HANKYU DEPARTMENT
STORES INC.**
㈱阪急百貨店

Department store / 百貨店
Product catalogue / 製品案内
1993
AD: Masaaki Kawai　川井正昭
AD, D: Tsuneya Tanaka　田中庸也
P: Yuichi Horie　堀江雄一
CW: Ryoko Hishida　菱田良子
size: 200×90 mm

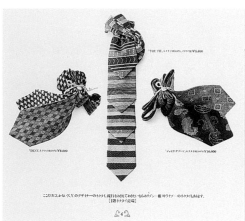

HANKYU DEPARTMENT •
STORES INC.

㈱阪急百貨店

Department store / 百貨店
Product catalogue / 製品案内
1995
CD: Masaaki Kawai　川井正昭
AD: Tsuneya Tanaka　田中庸也
D: Hiromi Fuzio　藤尾広美
P: Yuichi Horie　堀江雄一
CW: Yuriko Akao　赤尾 百合子
S: Hiroshi Ikushima　生島 寛
size: 180×210 mm

Retail • 089

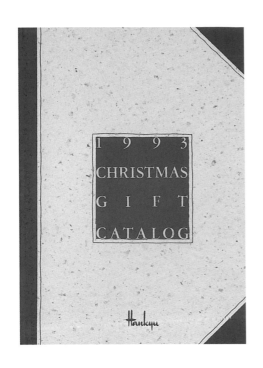

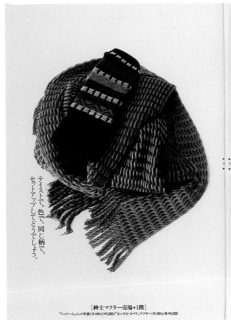

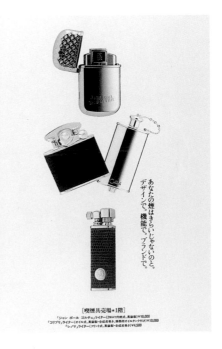

• **HANKYU DEPARTMENT
STORES INC.**

㈱阪急百貨店

Department store / 百貨店

Product catalogue / 製品案内

1993

CD: Tadao Sorori / Ryo Konishi

曽呂利 忠男 / 小西 良

AD: Tsuneya Tanaka　田中庸也

D: Tatsuya Nishimura　西村辰哉

P: Yuichi Horie　堀江雄一

CW: Kyoko Horiuchi　堀内杏子

S: Hiroshi Ikushima　生島 寛

size: 210×148 mm

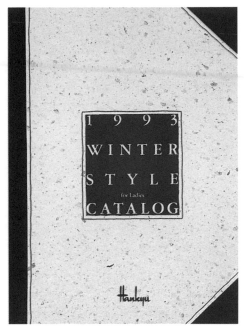

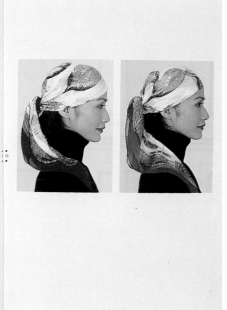

HANKYU DEPARTMENT •
STORES INC.
㈱阪急百貨店

Department store / 百貨店
Product catalogue / 製品案内
1993
CD: Tadao Sorori / Ryo Konishi
曽呂利 忠男 / 小西　良
AD: Tsuneya Tanaka　田中庸也
D: Hiromi Fuzio　藤尾広美
P: Yuichi Horie　堀江雄一
S: Hiroshi Ikushima　生島　寛
HM: Masashi Shimozi / HARIO　下地正史
size: 210×148 mm

- **THE SEIBU DEPARTMENT STORES, LTD.**
㈱西武百貨店

Department store / 百貨店

Product catalogue / 製品案内

1994

DF: Project Y　プロジェクト Y

size: 210×158 mm

ONE PIECES
Easy luxury

着まわし自在のワンピース。

1枚で、いくつものシーンをカバーするワンピース。素肌に
その肌ざわり、ブラウジングの重ね着をして、今夏に決まります。
流行のレースやボーダー、ワイドパンツを合わせて、
華やかなアクセサリーをそえて夜のドレスアップも。
組み合わせ次第で、
いろいろな着こなしを楽しめて、しかもリーズナブル。
春夏のおしゃれの必須アイテムです。

DINJU COLLECTIONS
FEMININITY · MODERN MARINE
COMBINATION WHITE · MIXING CULTURES

いまを感じとる、ディニューの新ライン。

女らしいシルエット、ディテールに凝ったデザイン、そしてトレンドへの
こだわり。新しい空気を敏感にキャッチして、いくつものシーンを描きだす、ディニュー。
春夏の新ラインにも、流行のきざしをみせるロマンティシズムが
あふれています。柔らかなパステルトーン、上質のデコラティブな生地、透ける素材の流れるようなライン。
もちろんディテールも、揺れるカフスや柔らかい衿が、トレンドを反映しています。
今シーズンの特長は、流動性・かろやかさ・透明感。
ディニューらしい鮮やかな色彩や個性的なプリントとともに、肩の力をぬいた
エアリーなスタイリングで、やさしい女らしさを表現します。

POLA COSMETICS INC. •

㈱ポーラ化粧品本舗

Cosmetics, fashion accessories
distributor / 化粧品等製造販売
Product catalogue / 製品案内
1994
CD: Masaharu Nakano（Dentsu）
中野雅春　㈱電通
AD, D: Diamond Head's
ダイアモンド・ヘッズ
P: Noboru Morikawa　森川　昇
CW: Keiko Sugiyama　杉山桂子
size: 297×220 mm

• SENSHUKAI CO., LTD.

㈱千趣会

Mail order retailer / 通信販売

Product catalogue / 製品案内

1994

CD, AD: Koji Kusatsugu　草次耕二

D: Tetsuya Takeuchi　竹内哲哉

P: Shunji Kaida　海田俊二

CW: Mutsuko Tanaka　田中睦子

DF: Studio VIS Co., Ltd.　㈱スタジオ ビス

size: 297×210 mm

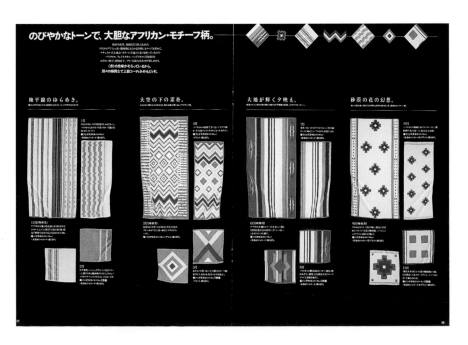

SENSHUKAI CO., LTD. •

㈱千趣会

Mail order retailer / 通信販売

Product catalogue / 製品案内

1993

CD, AD: Koji Kusatsugu　草次耕二

D: Kyoko Izumi / Tetsuya Takeuchi

泉　京子 / 竹内哲哉

P: Tsuyoshi Fuseya　伏谷　毅

CW: Mutsuko Tanaka　田中睦子

DF: Studio VIS Co., Ltd.　㈱スタジオ ビス

size: 345×257 mm

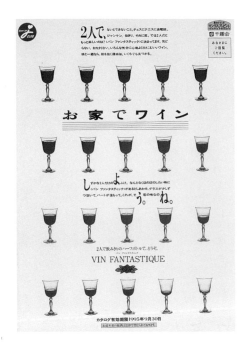

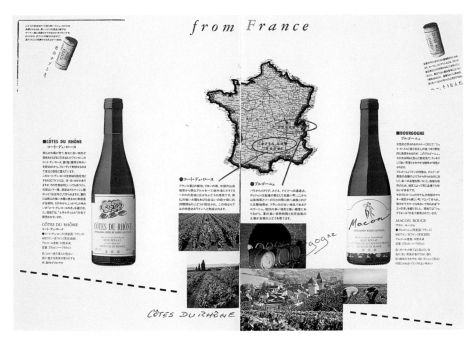

• **SENSHUKAI CO., LTD.**
㈱千趣会

Mail order retailer / 通信販売
Product catalogue / 製品案内
1995
CD, AD: Koji Kusatsugu　草次耕二
D: Tetsuya Takeuchi / Masae Kono
竹内哲哉 / 香野正恵
CW: Mutsuko Tanaka　田中睦子
DF: Studio VIS Co., Ltd.　㈱スタジオ ビス
size: 210×148 mm

無印良品
衣料品1995春

インディゴを洗う。
洗うことから生まれた新しい魅力の服たち。

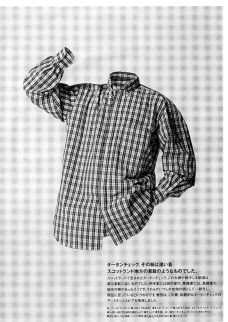

タータンチェック。その柄は遠い昔、
スコットランド地方の家紋のようなものでした。

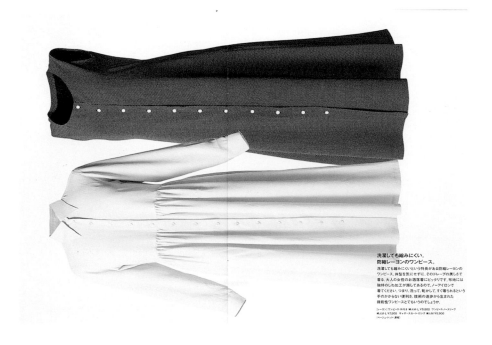

洗濯しても縮みにくい。
防縮レーヨンのワンピース。

RYOHINKEIKAKU CO., LTD. •

㈱良品計画

Product developer / 商品開発・販売

Product catalogue / 製品案内

1995

CD: Ikko Tanaka / Kazuko Koike

田中一光 / 小池一子

AD, D: Masaaki Hiromura　廣村正彰

D: Toshiyuki Kojima　小島利之

P: Takashi Oyama　大山　高

CW: Yoichi Umemoto　梅本洋一

DF: Hiromura Design Office, Inc.

廣村デザイン事務所

size: 257×185 mm

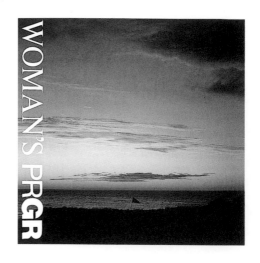

DATA
WOOD REVERSE

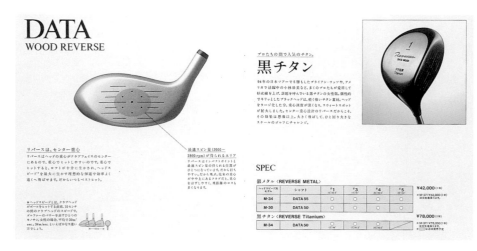

黒チタン

プロたちの間で人気のチタン。

94年の日本ツアーを制したグライアン・マッツや、アメリカで活躍中の小林浩美など、多くのプロたちが愛用して好成績を上げ、評価を高めている黒チタンですが。圧倒的なマチキャしたブラックヘッドは、軽い硬いチタン素材。ヘッドをシャープにしたり、重心深度が深くなり、スウィートスポットが拡大した。そのセンター重心設計のリバースだからこそ、その効果は倍増に上、大きく飛ばして、ひと回り大きなスケールのゴルフにチャレンジ。

リバースは、センター重心。

リバースはヘッドの重心がクラブフェイスのセンターにあるので、重心でヒットしやすいのです。重心でヒットすると、ソフトが十分に生かされ、ヘッドスピードを最大に生かす理想的な弾道で効率よく速く飛ばせるので、だからいつもベストヒット。

最適スピン量（2000～2800rpm）が得られるエリア

リバースはインパクトポイントと最適なスピン量の得られる位置がひとつになっているので、だから打ちやすい。だから飛ぶ。従来の設計がやや上にあるクラブでは、重心をはずしやすく、飛距離のロスも多くなります。

ヘッドスピードとは、クラブヘッドがボールをヒットする直前、10センチの間のクラブヘッドのスピードで、ミューの女性の場合の平均で30m／sec、24m/sec、といえばかなり速い方でしょう。

SPEC

鉄メタル（REVERSE METAL）
¥42,000（1本）

ヘッドスピード別 モデル	シャフト	#1 (11°/14.5°)	#3 (13°/16.5°)	#4 (14.5°)	#5	
M-34	DATA 55	○	○	○	○	※ M-27/¥42,000（1本）
M-30	DATA 50	○	○	○	○	次ブン発表予定

黒チタン（REVERSE Titanium）
¥78,000（1本）

M-34	DATA 50	○ (12°/15°)		○ (13°/16.5°)	○ (14.5°)		※ M-27/¥78,000（1本）
							次ブン発表予定

DATA
IRON

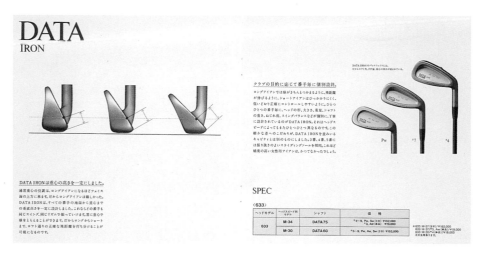

クラブの目的に応じて番手毎に個別設計。

DATA IRON は重心の高さを一定にしました。

通常重心の位置は、ロングアイアンになるほどフェイス面の上方に来ます。だからロングアイアンは難しかった。DATA IRON は、すべての番手の地面から重心までの高さを一定に設計しました。これならどの番手も同じスイングで同じように振っていけますし、同じ球をとらえることができます。だからロングからショートまで、ゴルフ通りの正確な飛距離を打ち分けることが可能になるのです。

SPEC

（633）

ヘッドモデル	ヘッドスピード別 モデル	シャフト	番手	価格
633	M-34	DATA75	#4～9、Pw、Sw（2本）	¥152,000
			#3、Aw（各本）	¥19,000
	M-30	DATA60	#5～9、Pw、Aw、Sw（2本）	¥152,000

μ-240i R.E.G.
レギュラースペック

飛びのイメージを変えてしまったウッドの名器ミュー240i。ヘッドスピードをコンセプトに、それぞれのゴルファーの個性に合わせて選べるミュー240iシリーズのレギュラースペックです。特にキャリアを積んだ女性ゴルファーに。

μ-240i E.L.S.
軽量スペック

パワーレベルの余り高くない女性でも思いきり振り切れて、飛ばしの快感を味わえる超軽量モデル。シャローフェイスヘッドなのでボールが上がりやすく、ラクに理想的な弾道を描いてドライブできます。大きな飛距離がとにかく魅力。

CT-535CP

異素材のヘッドを組み合わせたプロギアならではの複合感覚。4番から7番までカーボンヘッド。7番からSWまでステンレスヘッドと、7番をダブらせ密度の高い攻めを可能にしたセッティングです。まさに女性のために開発されたCPアイアン。

DATA 5000

飛びを重視したソフトツーピースと、超反発発カバーの採用で飛距離性能をアップしました。パッティングの感触もソフト。女性ゴルファーの平均的なヘッドスピードに合わせたM-30、軽く打ちたいビギナーにはM-34も。

M-30
¥7,200（1ダース）/ ¥600（1球）

• **THE YOKOHAMA RUBBER
CO., LTD.**

横浜ゴム㈱

Tires, sports goods supplier /
タイヤ・スポーツ用品メーカー

Product catalogue / 製品案内

1995

CD, CW: Yoshinari Nishimura　西村佳也

AD: Satoru Miyata　宮田　識

D: Eiki Hidaka / Mitsuo Hakozaki /

Makoto Yamamoto

日高英輝 / 箱崎充男 / 山本　誠

P: Tamotsu Fujii / Takahiro Kurokawa

藤井　保 / 黒川隆広

DF: Draft　ドラフト

size: 200×200 mm

SEVENPOCKETS

ぜんぶ、入りました。セブンポケット。

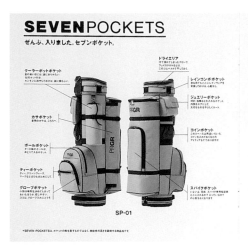

SP-01

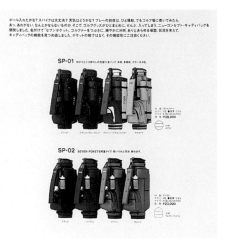

SOFT SPIKE for MEN

ひとこと、ラクです。

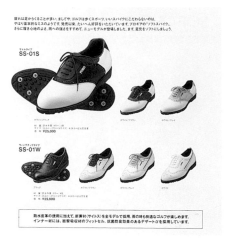

THE YOKOHAMA RUBBER •
CO., LTD.

横浜ゴム㈱

Tires, sports goods supplier /

タイヤ・スポーツ用品メーカー

Product catalogue / 製品案内

1995

CD, CW: Hiroshi Mitsui　三井　浩

AD: Hiroaki Nagai　永井裕明

D: Kyoko Ida　飯田京子

P: Tamotsu Fujii / Takahiro Kurokawa

藤井　保 / 黒川隆広

DF: N. G. Inc.　エヌ・ジー・インク

size: 200×200 mm

PRGR DATA SERIES

プロたちの間で人気のチタン。

黒チタン

'94年日本ツアーマスターズに勝ち星を重ねた
プラグアン・ウッドをはじめ、多くのプロたちが愛用して
好成績を上げ、話題をさらっているのが黒チタン。
慣性能で精悍なブラックヘッドは、いかやウッドのトレードマーク化。
軽くて黒いチタン素材の採用でヘッドが大型化。
重心深度が深くなって、その分スウィートスポットが拡大した。
センター重心設計のリバースがやさしく、
その効果は想像以上に大きい。

*1 HEAD SPEC
LOFT

FAIRWAY WOOD

リバースの重心インパクトの設計思想は、ティアップされないボールを打つ
スプーン、バフィ、クリークにこそ、むしろよく生かされている。
きちっと頭をとらえるフェアウエイウッドこそ、攻めの武器。
いよいよ待望の黒チタンのフェアウエイウッドも登場。

銀メタル

| #3 | #4 | #5 |

黒チタン

| #3 | #4 | #5 |

611

601 FORGED

軟鉄鍛造。プロに人気のキャビティアイアン。
日本のツアーで何人かのプロがこのアイアンを愛称ない
いかにも活躍をみせて話題になったもの。そのプロが使って
いるモデルを一般ゴルファーに公開。超精密鍛造製法に
よる高精度設計ヘッド。重心はDATA IRON 611に比べ
やや高く(ヒール方向)。同じいでもフィーリングが違う。プロ級
の高度な技術に支えられるやや高いニューキャビティ。
より高度な挑戦を求めるこだわり派のゴルファーたちに。

SPEC

611 & 622 CASTING

ヘッドモデル	ヘッドスピード別 モデル	シャフト	価格	
611	M-46	DATA 110	#3〜9, Pw, Aw, Sw (10本) ¥240,000	
	M-43	DATA 10S	#3〜9, Pw, Aw, Sw (各1本) ¥24,000	#2 (単品) ¥20,000
	M-40	標準シャフト DATA 100		
622	M-40	DATA 095		
	M-37	DATA 090	#3〜9, Pw, Aw, Sw (10本) ¥200,000	
	M-40	軽量シャフト DATA 080		
	M-37	DATA 075		

601 FORGED

| 601 | M-43 | 標準シャフト DATA 105 | #3〜9, Pw, Aw, Sw (10本) ¥280,000 | |
| | M-40 | DATA 100 | | |

BALL

飛びのツーピースを。スピンの糸巻きを。そんな固定観念はもう過去のものになった。
飛びもスピンもというニューツーピース DATA 7000 が登場したから。イメージ通り
思ったところにとまる。ピタッとピンにからみつく。今までのツーピースはもちろん、
他のソフトツーピースともキレアジがまるで違う。これはぜひひとつ比べてほしい。

DATA 7000

超ソフトスピンカバーを採用。ツーピースの飛距離に、糸巻き
ボールに近いスピン性能をプラスしたニューカテゴリーの
ツーピース。飛んでとまる。フィーリングも糸巻きに近く、
パッティングの感触もソフト。
M-43, M-40 ¥YB,400/1ダース ¥700/1球

DATA 5000

飛びを追究したソフトツーピース。超高反発カバーの採用
で飛距離性能をアップ。パワーヒッターから女性ゴルファー
まで、ヘッドスピードに合わせて最適のボールを選べるM-30、
M-34、M-37、M-40、M-43の5タイプ。
M-30, M-34, M-37, M-40, M-43 ¥Y7,200/1ダース ¥600/1球

• **THE YOKOHAMA RUBBER CO., LTD.**

横浜ゴム㈱

Tires, sports goods supplier /
タイヤ・スポーツ用品メーカー
Product catalogue / 製品案内
1995
CD, CW: Yoshinari Nishimura　西村佳也
AD: Satoru Miyata　宮田　識
D: Eiki Hidaka / Mitsuo Hakozaki /
Makoto Yamamoto
日高英輝 / 箱崎充男 / 山本　誠
P: Tamotsu Fujii / Takahiro Kurokawa
藤井　保 / 黒川隆広
DF: Draft　ドラフト
size: 200×200 mm

それは、あくまでも
プレイのための
ウェアである。

ゴルフを真正面からスポーツとして捉え直すとき、ゴルフウェアに一番求められているものは何よりも機能性だろう。最近のアメリカの若手プロたちのプレイスタイルを見ていると、それは明らかな流れだ。例えば夏のゴルフは汗が大敵である。しかしこれまで、この汗対策を科学的に、機能的に解決したウェアはなかった。こうした機能性を最優先させて開発されたのがドライシャツである。汗を追放し、軽さと動きを取り戻したドライシャフは、快適なプレイのための最もシンプルな哲学を持つゴルフウェアなのである。

PRGR
DRY SHIRTS

ゴルフ日和の DRY-1　汗ばむ季節の DRY-2

DRY CATEGORY

季節によっても汗の量は異なる。ドライシャフは変化する気温と汗の量を基準にして、ステージを「冷・快」「暖・暑」「酷暑」の三つに区分し、汗に対してそれぞれ異なった機能性を持つ3タイプのシャフを開発した。素材を変え、着想は季節を追って展開される。

〔冷・快〕　　〔暖・暑〕　　〔酷暑〕

PRGR DRY SHIRTS 1　PRGR DRY SHIRTS 2　PRGR DRY SHIRTS 3

THE YOKOHAMA RUBBER •
CO., LTD.

横浜ゴム㈱

Tires, sports goods supplier /

タイヤ・スポーツ用品メーカー

Product catalogue / 製品案内

1995

CD, CW: Yoshinari Nishimura　西村佳也

AD: Satoru Miyata　宮田 識

D: Eiki Hidaka / Mitsuo Hakozaki

日高英輝 / 箱崎充男

P: Tamotsu Fujii / Takahiro Kurokawa

藤井 保 / 黒川隆広

I: Norihisa Tojimbara　唐仁原 教久

DF: Draft　ドラフト

size: 200×200 mm

- **DESCENTE**

㈱デサント

Sports goods supplier /

スポーツ関連製品メーカー

Product catalogue / 製品案内

1995

CD, AD: Seigo Kaneko　金子正剛

D: Yoshiko Komatsubara　小松原 巧子

P: Takashi Oyama / Fumiya Kamakura

大山　高 / 鎌倉文也（ペンギン）

CW: Masayuki Minoda　蓑田雅之

size: 250×250 mm

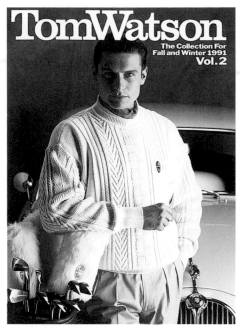

TomWatson
The Collection For
Fall and Winter 1991
Vol.2

**DUNLOP SPORTS •
ENTERPRISES**

㈱ダンロップ スポーツ エンタープライズ

Golf accessories manufacturer /

ゴルフ関連製品メーカー

Product catalogue / 製品案内

1991

CD, AD, D: Shinzo Fukui　福井信蔵

P: Koji Araki　荒木弘次

CW: Haruo Nakamura　中村晴夫

size: 355×245 mm

Sports • 103

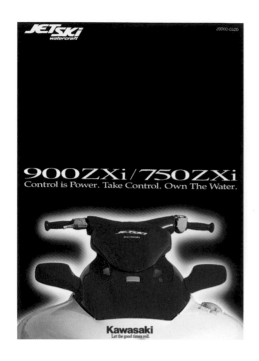

Control is Power

In Control
750ZXi

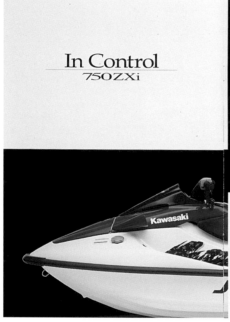

In Balance
900ZXi

- **KAWASAKI MOTORS CORPORATION JAPAN.**

  ㈱カワサキ モータース ジャパン

  Motor cycle, jet ski distributor /

  オートバイ・ジェットスキー販売

  Product catalogue / 製品案内

  1995

  CD: Taira Sakamoto　阪本　平

  AD, D: Yoichi Igarashi　五十嵐 陽一

  P: Rich Cox

  CW: Tetsuhiro Shibata　柴田 鉄博

  DF: Inter Image Inc. Advertising

  ㈱インターイメージ

  size: 297×210 mm

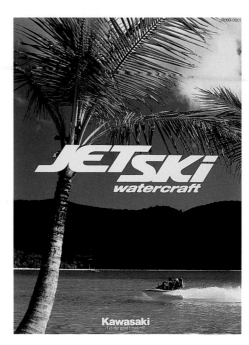

KAWASAKI MOTORS •
CORPORATION JAPAN.

㈱カワサキ モータース ジャパン

Motor cycle, jet ski distributor /
オートバイ・ジェットスキー販売

Product catalogue / 製品案内

1995

CD: Taira Sakamoto　阪本　平

AD, D: Yoichi Igarashi　五十嵐 陽一

P: Rich Cox

CW: Tetsuhiro Shibata　柴田鉄博

DF: Inter Image Inc. Advertising

㈱インターイメージ

size: 297×210 mm

Sports • 105

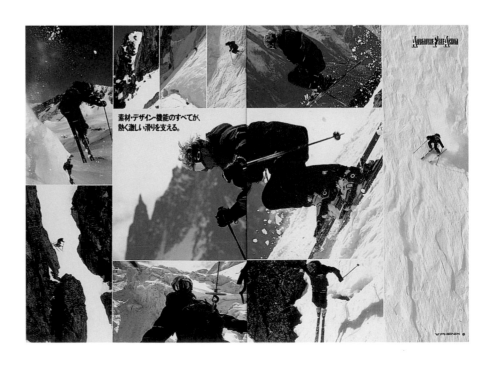

素材だけではない。ファッションにも　新たな進化がある。

● PHENIX

フェニックス

Sports goods supplier /

スポーツ関連製品メーカー

Product catalogue / 製品案内

1995

CD: Genyu Nakasone　仲宗根 玄雄

AD: Tetsuo Fujiwara　藤原哲男

D: Keisuke Fujiyama / Chizuru Sugihara

藤山啓介 / 杉原 ちづる

P: Kenji Kinoshita　木下健二

CW: Hitomi Nozu　能津 ひとみ

size: 364×257 mm

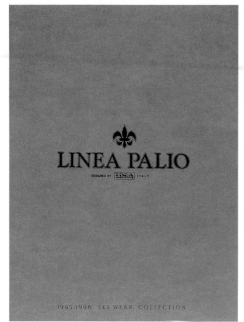

PHENIX •

フェニックス

Sports goods supplier /

スポーツ関連製品メーカー

Product catalogue / 製品案内

1995

CD: Genyu Nakasone　仲宗根 女雄

AD: Sadamichi Hayashi　林 貞通

D: Fumiko Arai / Chizuru Sugihara

荒井 富美子 / 杉原 ちづる

P: Peter Lindecke / Naohiro Isshiki

一色直弘

CW: Hitomi Nozu　能津 ひとみ

size: 364×257 mm

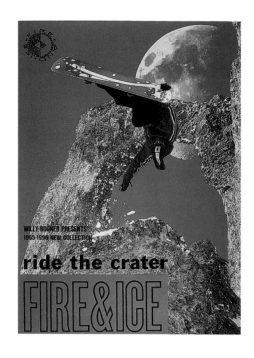

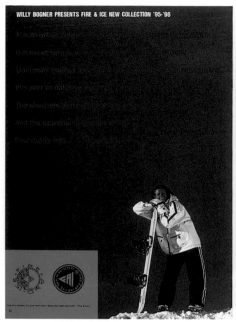

• **PHENIX**

フェニックス

Sports goods supplier /

スポーツ関連製品メーカー

Product catalogue / 製品案内

1995

CD: Genyu Nakasone　仲宗根 玄雄

AD: Tetsuo Fujiwara　藤原哲男

D: Fumiko Arai　荒井 富美子

P: Jean Marc Favre

CW: Yoichi Sekiguchi　関口洋一

size: 364×257 mm

GUM GUM INC. •

㈱ガムガム

Apparel maker / アパレル メーカー

Product catalogue / 製品案内

1995

CD: Hirofumi Kusumoto　楠本浩史

AD: Takaaki Yano　矢野孝明

P: Mikio Sugiura　杉浦幹雄

CW: Yoji Yamamoto　山本洋二

DF: Yohk Co.　ヨーク社㈲

size: 297×210 mm

Sports • 109

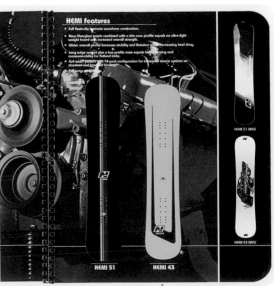

• **NITRO / PIAA CO.**

ナイトロ / PIAA ㈱

Snowboard manufacturer /
スノーボード メーカー

Product catalogue / 製品案内

1995

CD, AD, CW: Tommy Delago

D, I: Mike Kawson

P: Katja Delago

size: 297×245 mm

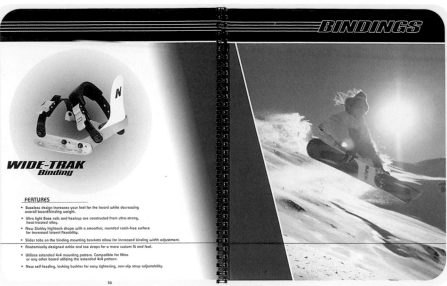

GROM
Binding

FEATURES

WIDE-TRAK
Binding

FEATURES

- Baseless design increases your feel for the board while decreasing overall board/binding weight.
- Ultra light Base rails and heelcup are constructed from ultra-strong, heat-treated alloy.
- New Stubby highback shape with a smoother, rounded catch-free surface for increased lateral flexibility.
- Slider tabs on the binding mounting brackets allow for increased binding width adjustment.
- Anatomically designed ankle and toe straps for a more custom fit and feel.
- Utilizes extended 4x4 mounting pattern. Compatible for Nitro or any other board utilizing the extended 4x4 pattern.
- New self-feeding, locking buckles for easy tightening, non-slip strap adjustability.

30

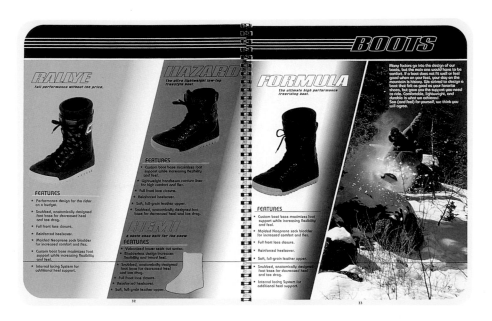

RALLYE
full performance without the price.

HAZARD
The ultra lightweight low-top freestyle boot.

FORMULA
The ultimate high performance freeriding boot.

Many factors go into the design of our boots, but the main one would have to be comfort. If a boot does not fit well or feel good when on your feet, your day on the mountain is history. We strived to design a boot that felt as good as your favorite shoes, but gave you the support you need to ride. Comfortable, lightweight, and durable is what we achieved. See (and feel) for yourself, we think you will agree.

FEATURES

FEATURES

FEATURES

HEMI
A skate shoe built for the snow.

FEATURES

32

33

RALLYE

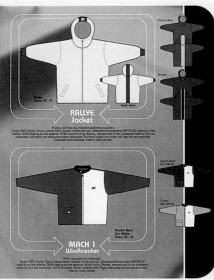

RALLYE
Jacket

MACH 1
Windbreaker

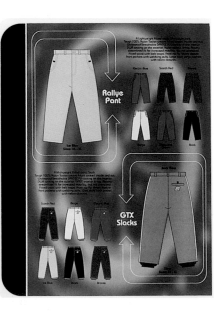

Rallye Pant

GTX Slacks

- **K2 SNOWBOARDS**

Snowboard manufacturer /

スノーボード メーカー

Product catalogue / 製品案内

1995

CD, AD, D, I, CW: Michael Strassburger

D, I, CW: Vittorio Costarella

D: George Estrada

P: Eric Berger / Jeff Curtes /

Aarron Sedway

I: Jimmy Clark / Yoshiro Higai

CW: Brent Turner / Luke Edgar

DF: Modern Dog

size: 278×210 mm

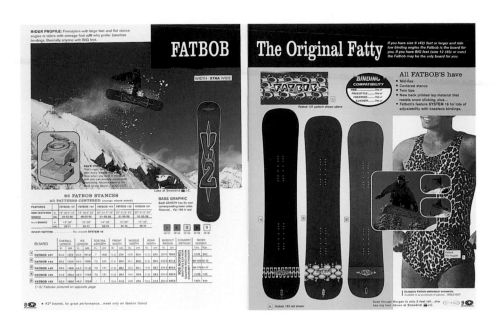

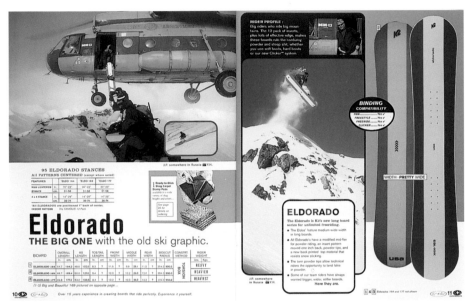

• **K2 SNOWBOARDS**

Snowboard manufacturer /

スノーボード メーカー

Product catalogue / 製品案内

1994

CD, AD, D, I, CW: Vittorio Costarella

CD: Brent Turner

CD, CW: Luke Edgar

D, I: Michael Strassburger

P: Jeff Curtes / Eric Berger /

Jules Frazier

CW: Hayley Martin

DF: Modern Dog

size: 280×105 mm

DESIGN PHILOSOPHY

All of us know exactly what it feels like when you're out in front in a race and really blasting, but if you can hear the smacking of your opponent's board on the water just behind you and you're straining and pushing for your rig to deliver just that much more power to go even further ahead.....

Because we know that feeling, we never stop for a minute with our commitment to R&D, our full-on efforts to make sure your Neil Pryde rig will deliver that extra power to keep you out in front, whether you're on the pro circuit or trying to outblast your friends on the local beach.

BETTER DESIGN TOOLS

Our unique CAD-CAM computer system for sail design enables our designers to create numerous generations of prototypes, relentlessly refining new concepts until they are integrated flawlessly into the overall function of the sail. The CAD-CAM system that controls panel cutting in our main production loft duplicates every panel of every sail with absolute precision, reproducing exactly the performance of the final prototypes.

APPROPRIATE TECHNOLOGY

Obviously we can't all be Dunkerbecks, or lucky enough to find every weekend at our local sailing spot delivering ideal World Cup conditions. Few of us will ever own the ultra-light, ultra-high-tech boards and fins that our top-of-the-line World Cup sails are designed to complement. That's why we're now spending a large proportion of our R&D on what we call "appropriate technology". Our best design minds are coming up with innovations that are every bit as sophisticated and smart as our World Cup high-tech, yet they're aimed at different solutions: how to get a sluggish production board blasting up onto a plane in marginal conditions, how to create a sail that has full-on power yet is RAF-easy to rig and effortless to handle, and so on. In our new 'Street' range, you can see and feel the benefits of this important extra direction in our design thinking.

Contents

1> Introduction
5> Technology
7> World Cup Concept
9> World Cup Slalom
11> World Cup Racing
13> Combat Wave
15> Street Racer
17> Street Slalom
19> 4WD
21> Gybe
23> Rig Integration
25> Carbon Masts
27> Booms & Bases
31> Specifications

World Cup Men's Overall Champion

Every sail in this range has been designed individually, refined, then re-refined to make it as close to perfect as possible for a specific set of racing conditions. The sole objective is to win course races in World Cup conditions, so the emphasis is inevitably on upwind performance, top-end speed on the long reaches and the capability to cope with fluctuating windspeeds over an extensive course. Spanier and Dunkerbeck have taken extra care to calibrate each sail to the type of water conditions encountered, together with the fin and board sizes used at a given wind strength. The World Cup Racing Mk III rigs are designed to be sailed fully loaded and can cope smoothly with overloading in big gusts. As a result, it's possible to use larger sizes than you would with other types of sail.

KEY DESIGN FEATURES

Spanier and Dunkerbeck worked with a highly evolved high-aspect, low drag foil shape and refined it to suit the specific requirements for each individual size. The following features are common to all the sails in the range.

- Relatively high aspect ratio, moderate boom length, narrow entry section tending towards flat and a shallow draft placed well back in the foil.

- Leech twist pattern emphasizes movement in the upper section of the leech.

- Tack radial panel shaping, five Supercans, tube-rod battens, step-up K-film and twin luff panels provide optimum foil shape, maximum aerodynamic efficiency and exceptional stability under load.

- Finishing details include the new Integral Tack Fairing, low friction tack fitting, new head finishing and tri-ply seaming.

- Must be used with the Carbon 60 mast.

SPANIER SPEAKS

Barry Spanier made these brief notes about the new sails and the achievements of the '92 generation of World Cup Racing sails they're derived from.

WCR 5.5: Emphasis on upwind speed overpowered. Has the flattest shape and fullest luff curve to create excellent leech tension and wide wind range.

WCR 5.7: 18-25 knots, pushing the edge of the course race standard. Developed as "a small 6.0" rather than "a large 5.5", this sail has increased high-end performance from its higher aspect planform and flatter shape.

WCR 6.0: Dominant size for course racing in 14-20 knot conditions. Has the best shape for control at very high board speeds. Bjorn and Britt have probably won every race they've entered using this design.

WCR 6.5: Amazing upwind, superfast reaching. Winning at the wind minimum by a 101 margin over second place. Both Britt and Bjorn came from deep in the pack to win every course race by minutes. Bjorn picked up 40 seconds on the second weather leg of the last race.

WCR 6.9: Developed in response to larger course/slalom boards for pushing the 11 knot World Cup minimum.

WCR 8.0: Built for wind minimum for Longboards. The design was first used in Holland in the fall of 1990. Bjorn has never lost a race using this sail. Nevin Sayre used it to win the US Open. Ten bullets.

The V8 Street Racer is a powerful engine designed specifically for production boards and 'local beach' conditions. Massive low-end acceleration gives it the capability to drive even the most sluggish production board straight onto a plane and get it powering to top speed. On a high-quality production board, the Street Racer becomes a seriously competitive rig. Like any great V8, this sail is crammed with advanced technology, but remains easy to tune and is built to last. If you're aggressively competitive – how many boardsailors aren't? – and basically just want to go flat out and beat everybody every time you step onto a board, this rig is for you.

DESIGN FEATURES

The Street Racer is built to provide devastating power with the emphasis on low-end acceleration and extra lift in light or gusting winds.

- A deep draft with a round entry and a controlled but smoothly twisting leech pumps out the basic power.

- Aerodynamic efficiency, refined shaping and enhanced foil stability guarantee maximum power output with minimum drag and makes the sail very easy to control. Designer Nils Rosenblad used three Supercans, a combination of Vert-X and tack radial seam shaping, tube-rod and speed section battens, and step-up K-film to achieve the best results.

- Turbocharging comes from the speed of the Carbon 25 flex response, which interacts with the other elements of the rig to create an Accelerating Power Cycle in overpowering conditions.

- Designed for use with the Carbon 25 Slalom mast, but can also be used with the Carbon 60.

NEW FOR 93

- The combined Vert-X /tack radial panel configuration.

- An additional Supercan – total is now three.

- New low-friction tack fitting.

- Integral tack fairing.

NEIL PRYDE •

Windsurfing equipment manufacturer /

ウィンドサーフィン関連製品メーカー

Product catalogue / 製品案内

1993

CD, AD, D: Byron Jacobs

DF: PPA Design Limited

size: 297×210 mm

Sports • 115

• NIKE ITALY S.R.L.

Sports goods supplier /
スポーツ関連製品メーカー
Product catalogue / 製品案内
1995
CD: Barbara Longiardi
AD: Emanuela Nanetti
CW: Antonella Bandoli
size: 215×105 mm

• NIKE ITALY S.R.L.

Sports goods supplier /
スポーツ関連製品メーカー
Product catalogue / 製品案内
1995
CD: Barbara Longiardi
AD: Emanuela Nanetti
P: Werther Scudellari
CW: Antonella Bandoli
size: 145×210 mm

NIKE ITALY S.R.L. •

Sports goods supplier /

スポーツ関連製品メーカー

Product catalogue / 製品案内

1995

CD: Barbara Longiardi

AD: Emanuela Nanetti

P: Werther Scudellari

CW: Antonella Bandoli

size: 148×149 mm

NIKE ITALY S.R.L. •

Sports goods supplier /

スポーツ関連製品メーカー

Product catalogue / 製品案内

1994

CD: Emanuela Nanetti /

Antonella Bandoli

P: Werther Scudellari

CW: Antonella Bandoli

size: 100×200 mm

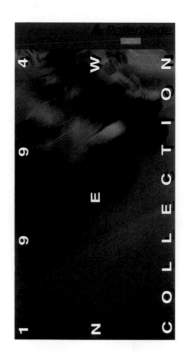

• **NORDICA JAPAN CO., LTD.**

日本ノルディカ㈱

Sports goods supplier /

スポーツ関連製品メーカー

Product catalogue / 製品案内

1993, 94

CD, CW: Kazuhiko Hachiya　八谷和彦

D: E. Galvani / Hiroto Kinoshita

木下博人

DF: SPAZIO Institute for Advanced

Thinking Inc.　㈱スパチオ研究所

size: 210×120 mm

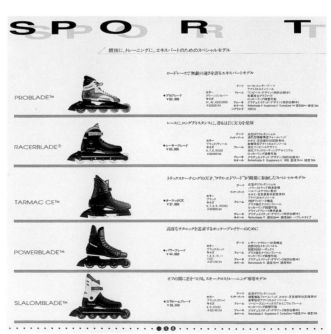

NORDICA JAPAN CO., LTD. •

日本ノルディカ㈱

Sports goods supplier /

スポーツ関連製品メーカー

Product catalogue / 製品案内

1993, 94

CD, CW: Kazuhiko Hachiya　八谷和彦

D: E. Galvani / Hiroto Kinoshita

木下博人

DF: SPAZIO Institute for Advanced

Thinking Inc.　㈱スパチオ研究所

size: 240×120 mm

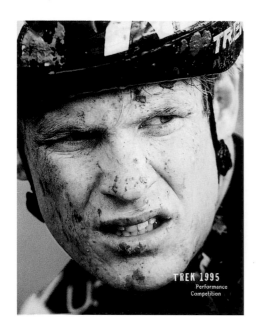

- **TREK BICYCLE**

  Cycle manufacturer / 自転車メーカー

  Product catalogue / 製品案内

  1995

  CD, AD: Joe Sutter

  D: Scott Schwebel

  P: Mark Salewsky

  I: Jon Hargreaves

  CW: Cheri Choudoir

  DF: Hanson / Dodge, Inc.

  size: 275×210 mm

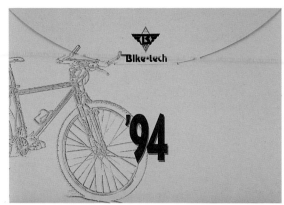

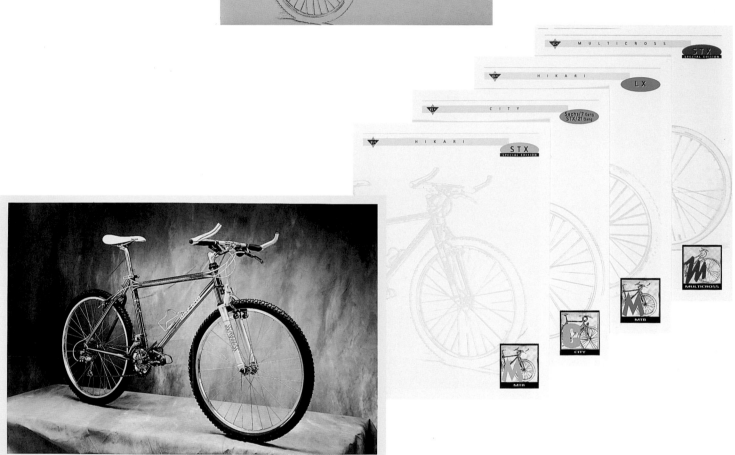

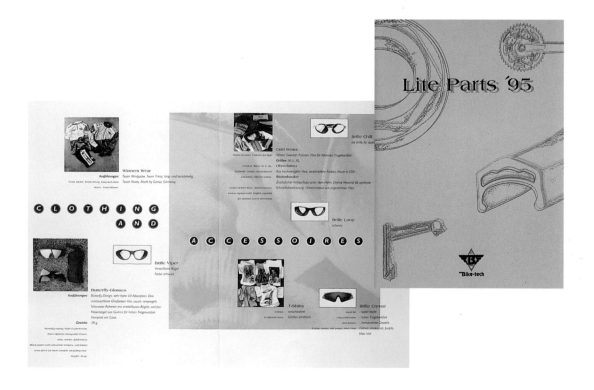

STORCK BIKE TECH •
TRADING

Cycle manufacturer / 自転車メーカー

Product catalogue / 製品案内

1994

CD, AD: Werner Liebchen

CD: Ilona Liebchen

AD: Wolfgang Wolker

P: Thomas Zörlein

DF: Liebchen + Liebchen

Grafik + Werbung GmbH

size: 190×260 mm

Sports • 121

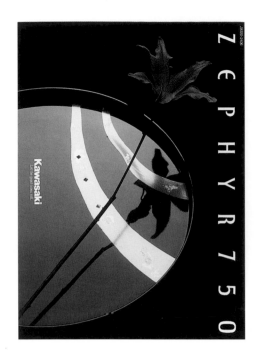

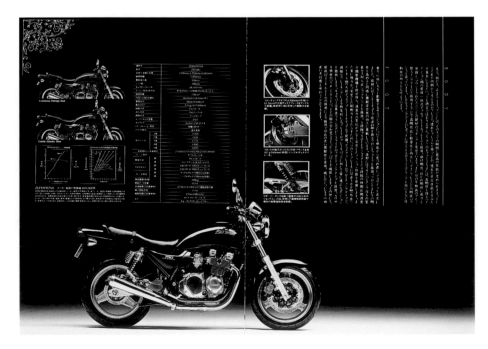

● **KAWASAKI MOTORS
CORPORATION JAPAN.**

㈱カワサキ モータース ジャパン

Motor cycle, jet ski distributor /
オートバイ・ジェットスキー販売
Product catalogue / 製品案内
1995
CD: Yatao Sasaki　佐々木 八太夫
AD, D: Tetsuya Kusuyama　楠山哲也
P: Shiromasa Kuyama　久山城正
CW: Katsunori Suzuki　鈴木克典
DF: AD Coordinate Co., Ltd.
㈱アドコーディネート
size: 297×210 mm

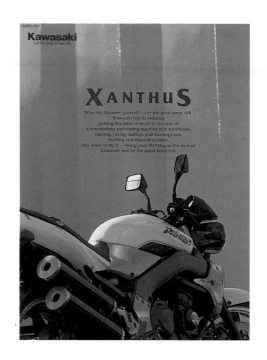

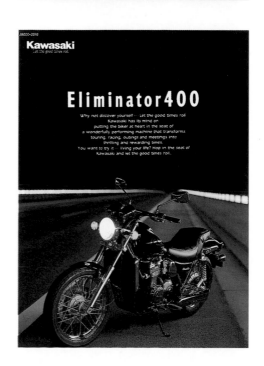

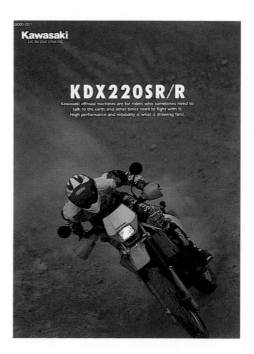

KAWASAKI MOTORS •
CORPORATION JAPAN.

㈱カワサキ モータース ジャパン

Motor cycle, jet ski distributor /

オートバイ・ジェットスキー販売

Product catalogue / 製品案内

1995

CD: Yatao Sasaki　佐々木 八太夫

AD, D: Tetsuya Kusuyama　楠山哲也

P: Shiromasa Kuyama　久山城正

CW: Katsunori Suzuki　鈴木克典

DF: AD Coordinate Co., Ltd.

㈱アドコーディネート

size: 297×210 mm

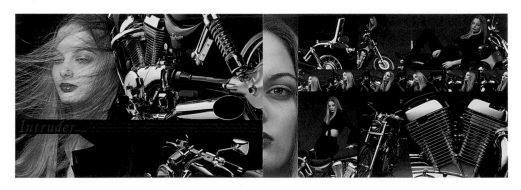

- **SUZUKI MOTOR
CORPORATION**

  スズキ㈱

  Auto maker / 自動車メーカー

  Product catalogue / 製品案内

  1993

  CD: Toshihiro Sawayanagi　沢柳敏宏

  AD: Kazuya Kubo　久保和也

  D: Eiji Hodono / Takaya Godo

  程野栄治 / 郷渡隆哉

  P: Yoshiro Kashiwagi　柏木善郎

  CW: Shinichi Kajiwara　梶原慎一

  DF: Hakuhodo Incorporated　㈱博報堂

  size: 297×210 mm

天を駆け、地を制す。

RMX250S

SUZUKI MOTOR •
CORPORATION

スズキ㈱

Auto maker / 自動車メーカー

Product catalogue / 製品案内

1995

CD: Masashi Kudo　工藤雅史

AD: Masaya Hirata　平田雅也

D: Yoshinori Hiraide　平出義則

P: Yasuhiro Tanaka　田中康裕

CW: Seiichi Yoshii　吉井省一

DF: N. C. S., Advertising Inc.

㈱エヌ・シー・エス アドバタイジング

size: 297×210 mm

Vehicles • 125

• **SUZUKI MOTOR
CORPORATION**

スズキ㈱

Auto maker / 自動車メーカー

Product catalogue / 製品案内

1995

CD: Toshihiro Sawayanagi　沢柳敏宏

AD: Kazuya Kubo　久保和也

D: Michihide Nishiiri　西入道秀

P: Koji Sasaki / Michio Hori

佐々木 香児 / 堀　道雄

CW: Shinichi Kajiwara　梶原慎一

DF: Hakuhodo Incorporated　㈱博報堂

size: 297×210 mm

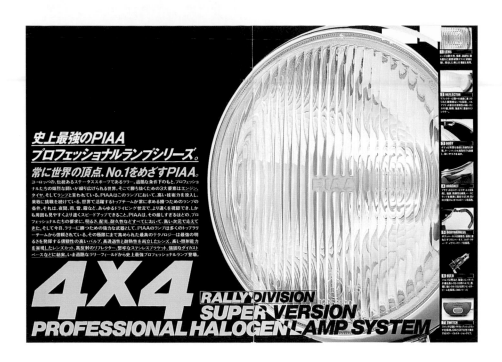

PIAA CORPORATION •

PIAA㈱

Auto accessories manufacturer /

自動車用品メーカー

Product catalogue / 製品案内

1994

CD, AD, D: Teruaki Yamamoto　山本昭明

size: 364×257 mm

自由・自在
RV ラシーン
ポイントブック

RASHEEN

HELLO!

RASHEEN

僕たちの、自由自在RVが生まれたよ。

名前はラシーン。羅針盤からもらったんだ。

DOKODEMO DOOR

NEW CONCEPT
RV

RVで、こんなコトしたいな。あんなトコ行きたいな。

だから、ラシーンは考えたんだ。RVにホントに必要なものってなんだろう？

FULL AUTO FULL TIME
4WD

OPTION

まずは、どこでも行けちゃうのもしい足まわりでしょ。

ワクワクしちゃう、遊び道具がいっぱい。これも大切。

• **NISSAN MOTOR CORPORATION**

日産自動車㈱

Auto maker / 自動車メーカー

Product catalogue / 製品案内

1994

CD: Teruhiko Ando / Makoto Fukuju

安藤輝彦 / 福寿 誠

AD: Shinobu Okouchi / Akio Sakashita

大河内 忍 / 坂下晶夫

D: Michinao Suzuki 鈴木通直

P: Yoshiro Kashiwagi / Isamu Kasai /

Junichiro Nishimaki / Jun Takahashi /

Yukikazu Ito

READER'S CARD

Thank you for purchasing a fine P·I·E Books publication. We would appreciate it very much if you would take a moment to complete the following questionnaire and return it to us so that we can keep you up to date on our latest releases. We will use the information you provide as our inspiration for future projects.

BOOK TITLE: ## Catalog & Pamphlet Collection 3

1. Let us know what you think of this particular book. Tell us what themes you would like us to handle in future.

How I liked this book:

Themes I am interested in:

2. How did you discover this book?

A. Heard about it from a friend   B. Saw it in the bookstore

C. Read about it in another P·I·E publication   D. Received notice by direct mail

E. Other (   )

3. Have you ever returned a reader's card to P·I·E before?

A. Yes   B. No

NAME

OCCUPATION   AGE

COMPANY

STREET

CITY

STATE   ZIP   COUNTRY

TEL.   FAX.

e-mail

Please

affix

postage

P·I·E BOOKS

#301, 4-14-6 Komagome, Toshima-ku
Tokyo 170-0003
Japan

It's new!

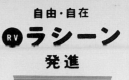

自由・自在

RV ラシーン

発進

RASHEEN

RVに本当に必要なものって何だろう？

It's simple!

TYPE I

TYPE II

TYPE III

BODY COLOR & SEAT

遊べる自由、遊べる自由、組み合わせる自由。
さあ、自分らしさでチョイスしよう。

NISSAN MOTOR CORPORATION •

日産自動車㈱

Auto maker / 自動車メーカー

Product catalogue / 製品案内

1994

CD: Teruhiko Ando / Makoto Fukuju

安藤輝彦 / 福寿　誠

AD: Shinobu Okouchi / Akio Sakashita

大河内　忍 / 坂下晶夫

D: Michinao Suzuki　鈴木通直

P: Yoshiro Kashiwagi / Isamu Kasai

Junichiro Nishimaki / Jun Takahashi

Yukikazu Ito

- **MAZDA MOTOR CORPORATION**

  マツダ㈱

  Auto maker / 自動車メーカー

  Product catalogue / 製品案内

  1995

  CD: AD International Inc.

  ㈱アドインターナショナル

  AD: Futoshi Someya　染谷　太

  D: Jun Osawa / Kazuo Aono

  大澤　純 / 青野一夫

  P: Eiji Nishizawa　西澤永治

  CW: Kazunori Kurematsu　樽松一憲

  size: 280×280 mm

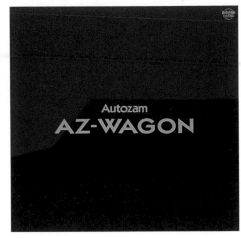

AUTOZAM INC., •

㈱オートザム

Auto dealer / 自動車ディーラー

Product catalogue / 製品案内

1994

CD: Naoko Harada　原田尚子

AD: Isamu Oteki　樗木　勇

D: Masato Yamada　山田政人

P: Ichiro Ebisawa　海老澤　一郎

CW: Yasuyuki Morishita　森下康幸

size: 280×280 mm

Vehicles • 131

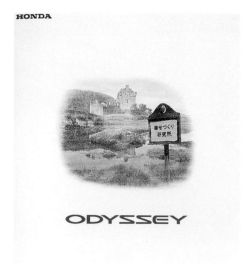

ODYSSEY

幸せづくり研究所。

ユカイもカイテキも楽々超えた。オデッセイ。

● **HONDA MOTOR CO., LTD.**

本田技研工業㈱

Auto maker / 自動車メーカー

Product catalogue / 製品案内

1994

CD: Taisuke Okano　岡野泰輔

AD: Seiichi Ohashi　大橋清一

D: Hiroyuki Itonaga / Hiroyuki Ito

糸永浩之 / 伊藤弘行

P: Naoki Tsuruta　鶴田直樹

CW: Ichiro Sugitani　杉谷一郎

DF: Les Mains Inc.　ＣＣ ㈱レマン

size: 297×245 mm

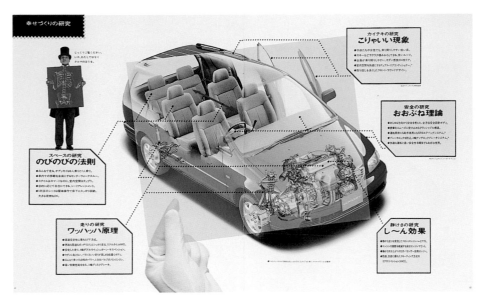

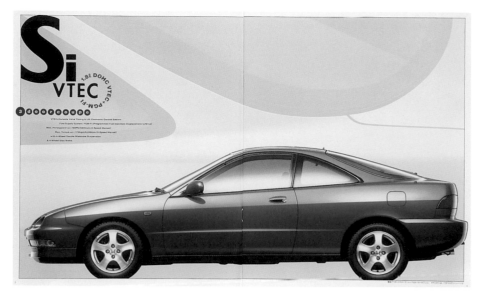

• **HONDA MOTOR CO., LTD.**

本田技研工業㈱

Auto maker / 自動車メーカー

Product catalogue / 製品案内

1993

CD, AD: Seiichi Ohashi　大橋清一

D: Masaru Hayashi / Hiroyuki Itonaga

林　勝 / 糸永浩之

P: Yoshiharu Asayama　朝山議晴

CW: Ichiro Sugitani　杉谷一郎

DF: Les Mains Inc.　ＣＣ㈱レマン

size: 297×245 mm

知性を感じさせる新鮮なデザイン、
ヨーロッパの香りがするエレガントなたたずまいです。

Type X

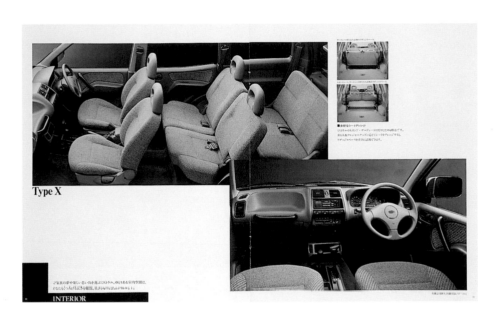

Type X

ご家族の夢や楽しい思い出を育むミストラル。ゆとりある室内空間は、
どなたにもくつろげる広さ、機能性、居心地のよさが備わっています。

INTERIOR

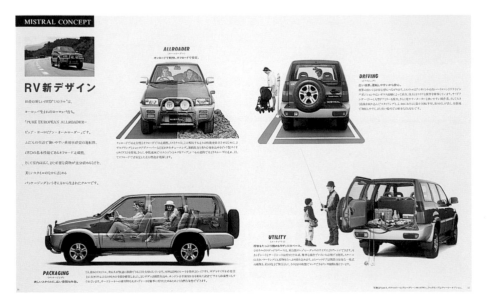

MISTRAL CONCEPT

RV新デザイン

日産の新しい4WDミストラルは、
ヨーロッパ生まれのヨーロッパ育ち。

「PURE EUROPEAN ALLROADER」

ピュア・オーロピアン・オールローダーです。

ALLROADER

DRIVING

UTILITY

PACKAGING

NISSAN MOTOR CORPORATION •

日産自動車㈱

Auto maker / 自動車メーカー

Product catalogue / 製品案内

1994

PR: Yukihiro Mukae　向江征洋

CD: Nissan Graphic Arts

日産グラフィックアーツ

AD, D: Hideki Hori　堀　秀樹

P: Yukio Shimizu　清水幸雄

CW: Katsuhiko Takeuchi　竹内克彦

size: 297×245 mm

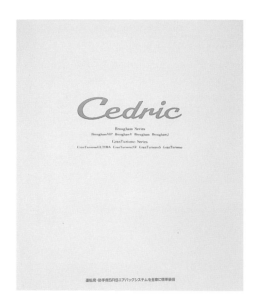

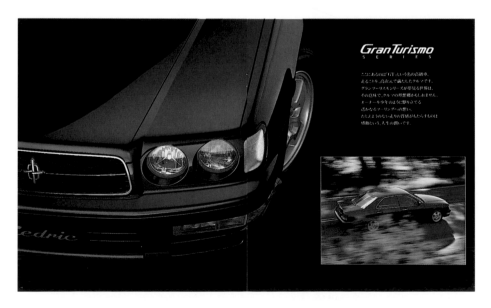

- **NISSAN MOTOR CORPORATION**

日産自動車㈱

Auto maker / 自動車メーカー

Product catalogue / 製品案内

1995

PR: Yutaka Oki　大木　豊

CD: Nissan Graphic Arts

日産グラフィックアーツ

AD, D: Shunichiro Mihara　三原　俊一郎

P: Hiroyuki Ozaki　尾崎洋行

CW: Kiichi Watanabe　渡辺帰一

size: 297×245 mm

スポーツカーに乗ろうと思う。

Version S シリーズ新登場。

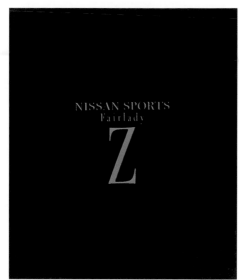

NISSAN SPORTS
Fairlady
Z

Version S・RECARO Twin Turbo 2by2

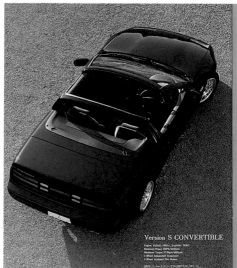

Version S CONVERTIBLE

Z MECHANISM

NISSAN MOTOR CORPORATION •

日産自動車㈱

Auto maker / 自動車メーカー

Product catalogue / 製品案内

1994

PR: Toshiaki Sekine　関根俊明

CD: Nissan Graphics Arts

日産グラフィックアーツ

AD, D: Kazuhiro Sueda　末田和博

P: Makoto Kashiwabara　柏原　誠

CW: Kiichi Watanabe　渡辺帰一

size: 297×245 mm

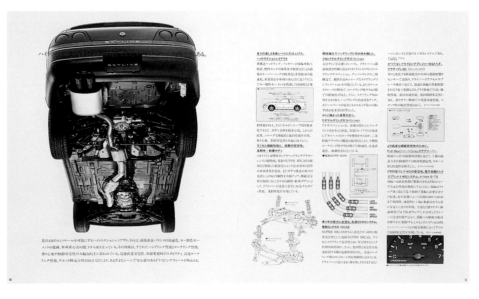

- **NISSAN MOTOR CORPORATION**

日産自動車㈱

Auto maker / 自動車メーカー

Product catalogue / 製品案内

1995

PR: Taichi Yamaguchi　山口太一

CD: Nissan Graphic Arts

日産グラフィックアーツ

AD: Ryoichi Shibuya　渋谷良一

D: Masakatsu Toki　土岐正勝

P: Koji Baba　馬場孝治

CW: Hikaru Yamaai　山合　光

DF: Bark Corporation　㈱バーク

size: 297×245 mm

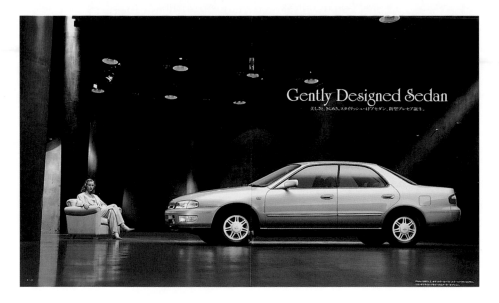

Gently Designed Sedan

美しさし、きらめき。スタイリッシュ・4ドアセダン、新型プレセア誕生。

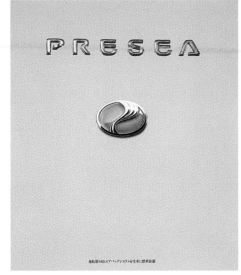

P R E S E A

運転席SRSエアバッグシステム全車に標準装備

Ct.II

Comfortable Equipment

本当に運転がしやすい。ほれぼれするクルマがここにある。

4.9 m

NISSAN MOTOR CORPORATION •

日産自動車㈱

Auto maker / 自動車メーカー

Product maker / 製品案内

1995

PR: Toshiaki Sekine　関根俊明

CD: Nissan Graphic Arts

日産グラフィックアーツ

AD, D: Hideki Hori　堀 秀樹

P: Koji Baba　馬場孝治

CW: Masao Kumagami　熊耳正雄

size: 297×245 mm

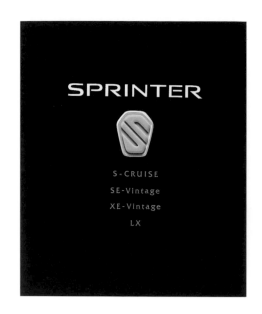

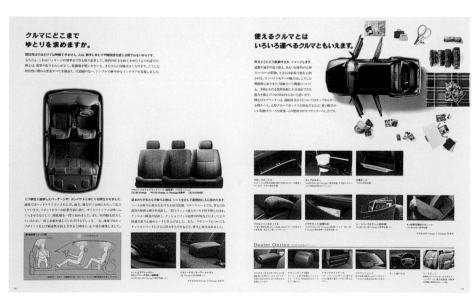

- **TOYOTA MOTOR CORPORATION**

  トヨタ自動車㈱

  Auto maker / 自動車メーカー

  Product catalogue / 製品案内

  1995

  DF: Nippon Design Center Inc.

  ㈱日本デザインセンター

  size: 297×245 mm

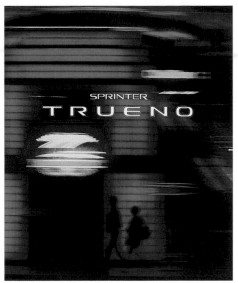

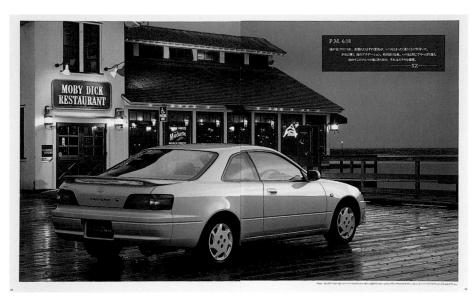

**TOYOTA MOTOR •
CORPORATION**

トヨタ自動車㈱

Auto maker / 自動車メーカー

Product catalogue / 製品案内

1995

DF: Nippon Design Center Inc.

㈱日本デザインセンター

size: 297×245 mm

Vehicles • 141

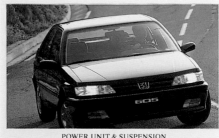

POWER UNIT & SUSPENSION

SAFETY

• INCHCAPE PEUGEOT
JAPAN CO., LTD.

インチケープ・プジョー ジャパン㈱

Auto dealer / 自動車ディーラー

Product catalogue / 製品案内

1994

CD: Haruo Yoshida　吉田春雄

AD: Norio Kudo　工藤規雄

D: Naoto Fujiwara / Yoshifumi Hioki

藤原直人 / 日置好文

P: Naoki Nishi / Takahito Sato

西　直樹 / 佐藤孝仁

CW: Naotoshi Shimosato　下里尚利

DF: I & S Corporation /
Magna, Inc. Advertising

㈱アイアンドエス / ㈱マグナ

size: 297×256 mm

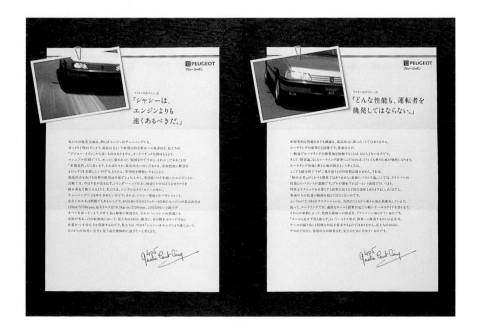

INCHCAPE PEUGEOT •
JAPAN CO., LTD.

インチケープ・プジョー ジャパン㈱

Auto dealer / 自動車ディーラー

Product catalogue / 製品案内

1994

CD: Haruo Yoshida　吉田春雄

AD: Norio Kudo　工藤規雄

D: Naoto Fujiwara / Yoshifumi Hioki

藤原直人 / 日置好文

P: Yoshifumi Ogawa / Masahiro Kato /

Naoki Nishi

小川義文 / 加藤正博 / 西　直樹

CW: Naotoshi Shimosato　下里尚利

DF: I & S Corporation /

Magna, Inc. Advertising

㈱アイアンドエス / ㈱マグナ

size: 297×210 mm

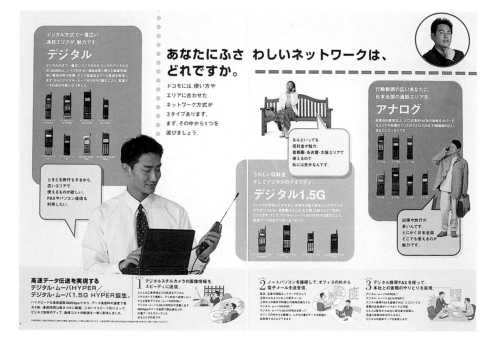

• **NTT MOBILE COMMUNICATIONS NETWORK INC.**

NTT 移動通信網㈱

Telecommunications / 電信電話

Product catalogue / 製品案内

1995

CD: Kimiaki Deguchi　出口公明

AD: Tsuyoshi Sato　佐藤　剛

D: Takeshi Sobukawa　曽武川 猛

P: Yutaka Myoshoji / Hikaru Kobayashi

明正寺 豊 / 小林　光

I: Katsuaki Mukai　向井勝明

CW: Kazuhisa Ishikawa / Chinatsu Seko

石川一久 / 瀬古千夏

DF: Taki Corp.　たき工房

size: 297×210 mm

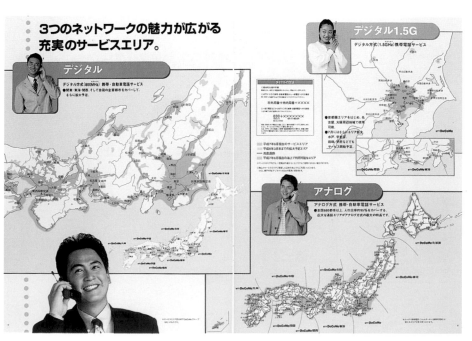

というあなたに、ツーといえばカー。
ツーカーは大幅値下げしました

選べる料金プランで、はっきり差がつく通話料。余裕だね。
平日昼間、東京から名古屋まで
1分間で60円！

ツーカー携帯電話

1.5GHz PDC方式
総合カタログ
1995/6

tu-ka

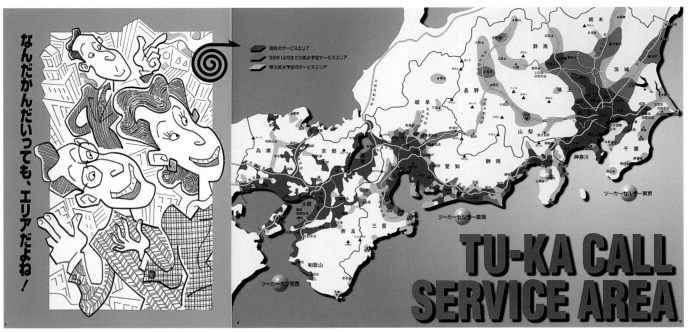

なんだかんだいっても、エリアだよね！

TU-KA CALL
SERVICE AREA

携帯といっても電話だけじゃネ。

というあなたに、ツーといえばカー。
ツーカーのデータ通信

FAX・パソコンはもちろん、
デジタルスチルカメラとの接続もOK。
ツーカーはまさに
マルチメディア端末だ。

急速に成長するマルチメディア社会。
そのキーとなるのが、デジタルのツーカー。

**TU-KA CELLULAR •
TOKYO INC.**

㈱ツーカーセルラー 東京

Telecommunications / 電信電話
Product catalogue / 製品案内
1995
CD, AD: Masayuki Shimizu　清水正行
D: Taku Wakabayashi　若林 卓
P: Akira Ogasawara　小笠原 昌
I: Kazunori Kanda　神田和則
CW: Gimpei Sato　佐藤銀平
size: 297×210 mm

Electrical equipment • 145

- **KENWOOD CORPORATION**

㈱ケンウッド

Electrical equipment manufacturer /
電気機器メーカー

Product catalogue / 製品案内

1995

CD: Osamu Hongo / Yoshiaki Matsueda
本郷　修 / 松枝良明

AD, CW: Yasumasa Fujita　藤田泰正

AD: Hideki Kihara　木原秀樹

D: Yoshiyuki Matsuyama　松山佳幸

P: Kyoji Takahashi / Masayuki Yamanaka
高橋恭司 / 山中政行

size: 297×210 mm

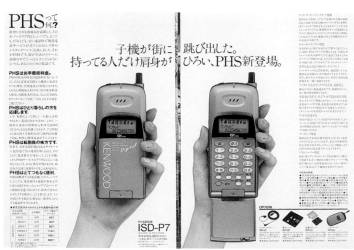

YAMAHA •

ヤマハ

Audio equipment manufacturer /

オーディオ機器等メーカー

Product catalogue / 製品案内

1994

CD, AD: Masahiko Uki　卯木正彦

D: Mitsuyo Akiba　秋葉光世

P: Tamotsu Kawaguchi　川口 保

CW: Christopher Williams

DF: Mum House　マム ハウス

size: 280×210 mm

• **MATSUSHITA ELECTRIC INDUSTRIAL CO., LTD.**

松下電器産業㈱

Electrical equipment manufacturer /
電気製品メーカー

Product catalogue / 製品案内

1995

AD: Nobuharu Takanishi　高西信治

D: Atsuya Kanamori　金森篤也

P: Masashi Ono　小野雅士

I: Illustration Bank
イラストレーション Bank

CW: Kenji Misumi　三隅健二

DF: Gothic Inc.　㈱ゴシック

size: 297×210 mm

SHARP CORPORATION •

シャープ㈱

Electrical equipment manufacturer /
電気製品メーカー

Product catalogue / 製品案内

1994, 95

AD: Yoshiaki Kobayashi　小林義明

D: Toshimitsu Takeuchi　竹内利光

P: Hideo Asai　浅井秀夫

CW: Mari Urakawa　浦川真理

size: 297×210 mm

MATSUSHITA ELECTRIC INDUSTRIAL CO., LTD. •

松下電器産業㈱

Electrical equipment manufacturer / 電気製品メーカー

Product catalogue / 製品案内

1993

AD: Nobuharu Takanishi　高西信治

D: Atsuya Kanamori　金森篤也

P: Daisuke Iryo　井料大助

CW: Hiroshi Onishi　大西博司

DF: Gothic Inc.　㈱ゴシック

size: 297×210 mm

• **MATSUSHITA ELECTRIC
INDUSTRIAL CO., LTD.
AUDIO DIVISION**

松下電器産業㈱オーディオ事業部

Audio equipment manufacturer /

オーディオ機器メーカー

Product catalogue / 製品案内

1994

CD: Toshihiko Ozaki　尾崎俊彦

AD: Takaharu Hara　原　孝治

D: Katsuhiro Takizawa　瀧澤勝弘

P: Ernst Haas / Taishi Hirokawa /

Masaaki Miyazawa / Kenji Ishikawa /

Toshinobu Kobayashi / Toru Inoue

広川泰士 / 宮澤正明 / 石川賢治 /

小林敏伸 / 井上　透

CW: Toshihiko Ozaki / Kei Nakayama

尾崎俊彦 / 中山　計

DF: ZOOM Inc.　㈱ズーム

size: 297×210 mm

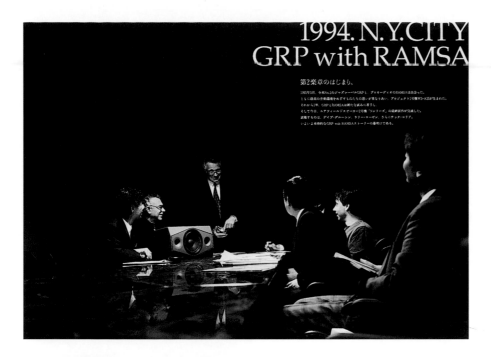

1994. N.Y.CITY
GRP with RAMSA

第2楽章のはじまり。

1994年3月、今世紀最大のジャズレーベル「GRP」と、プロオーディオの「RAMSA」は出会った。
そして最高の音楽機器をめざすものたちの思いが重なりあい、プロジェクト「号機WS-A35」が生まれた。
それから2年、「GRP&RAMSA」は新たな試みに書けた。
そして今日、ニアフィールドスピーカー「Nシリーズ」の最終試作機が完成した。
試聴するのは、デイブ・グルーシン、ラリー・ローゼン、うにチック・コリア。
いよいよ本格的なGRP with RAMSAスピーカーの幕開けである。

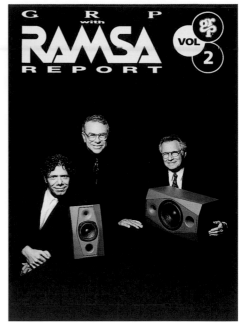

Chick Corea
チック・コリア

What I'm Seeking is Warm Sounds.

私がさがしているのは、あったかい音だ。

Near Field Speaker
WS-N20

Near Field Speaker
WS-N40

Larry Rosen
ラリー・ローゼン

Depth! Transparency! Great Job!

深い！透明だ！すごい仕事だ！

Near Field Speaker
WS-N40

**MATSUSHITA •
COMMUNICATION
INDUSTRIAL CO., LTD.**

松下通信工業㈱

Electrical equipment manufacturer /

電気機器メーカー

Product catalogue / 製品案内

1994

CD: Yoichi Miura　三浦洋一

AD: Osamu Takeuchi　竹内オサム

P: Mark Higashino　マーク 東野

CW: Hironori Nakajima　中嶋宏典

DF: Creators Group MAC / ZOOM Inc.

㈱クリエイターズグループ MAC / ㈱ズーム

size: 297×210 mm

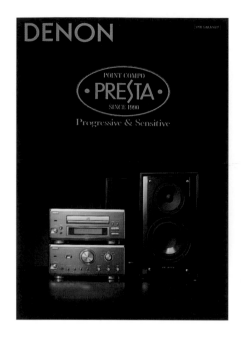

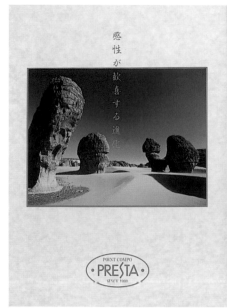

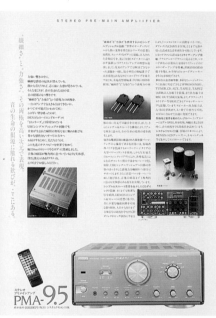

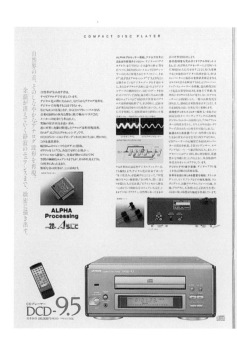

- **NIPPON COLUMBIA CO., LTD.**

日本コロムビア㈱

Electrical equipment manufacturer /
オーディオ機器メーカー

Product catalogue / 製品案内

1995

AD: Toru Shigeyama　重山 徹

D: Yumiko Kunugi　功力 由美子

P: Yasuo Akita / Shigeru Teruuchi
秋田恭男 / 照内 潔

CW: Koichi Shimizu　清水耕一

DF: C & D / Landmark Inc.
㈱ C & D / ㈱ランドマーク

size: 297×210 mm

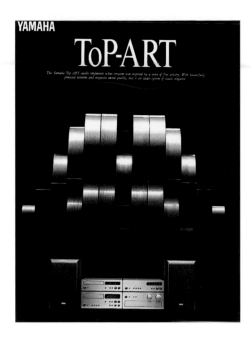

YAMAHA •

ヤマハ

Audio equipment manufacturer /

オーディオ機器等メーカー

Product catalogue / 製品案内

1995

CD, AD: Masahiko Uki　卯木正彦

D: Kimiaki Sato　佐藤公章

P: Naohiro Isshiki　一色直裕

CW: Hisaharu Miyazaki　宮崎久晴

O: Takenobu Igarashi　五十嵐 威暢

DF: Mum House　マムハウス

size: 280×210 mm

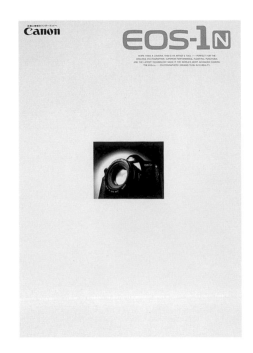

• **CANON SALES INC.**

キヤノン販売㈱

Precision equipment distributor /

精密機器販売

Product catalogue / 製品案内

1994

CD: Masaru Tanaka　田中　勝

AD: Kenji Inoue　井上健司

D: Yukio Kurosawa　黒沢幸雄

P: Chikao Todoroki　轟　近夫

CW: Kazuhiro Imai　今井和浩

size: 297×210 mm

時代を見抜き、人間を見つめ、自然を見続ける。
写真がもっと、写真らしくあるために。
まったく新しいEOSの誕生です。

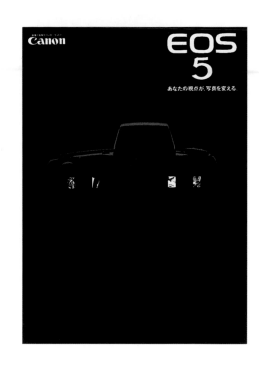

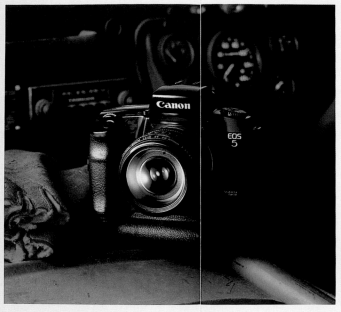

あなたの感動が、そのまま映像になる「EOS 5誕生。」

最新鋭テクノロジーが、AF一眼をここまで高めた、高精度AE。

CANON SALES INC. •

キャノン販売㈱

Precision equipment distributor /

精密機器販売

Product catalogue / 製品案内

1992

CD: Masaru Tanaka　田中　勝

AD: Kenji Inoue　井上健司

D: Sumie Yamada　山田澄江

P: Chikao Todoroki　轟　近夫

CW: Kazuhiro Imai　今井和浩

size: 297×210 mm

Electrical Equipment • 155

• **MINOLTA CO., LTD.**

ミノルタ㈱

Precision equipment manufacturer /

精密機器メーカー

Product catalogue / 製品案内

1994

CD: Yasuyuki Ito　伊藤康幸

AD: Minoru Nakamura　中村　実

D: Mari Seike　清家真理

P: Ken Takahara　高原　健

CW: Tatsuo Tanaka　田中建夫

size: 297×210 mm

MINOLTA CO., LTD. •

ミノルタ㈱

Precision equipment manufacturer /

精密機器メーカー

Product catalogue / 製品案内

1994

CD: Shinkichi Osugi / Yasuyuki Ito

大杉新吉 / 伊藤康幸

AD: Shoji Ebihara　海老原 摂治

D: Hidenori Kurashina　蔵品秀典

P: Ken Takahara　高原 健

CW: Dai Some　荘目 大

size: 297×210 mm

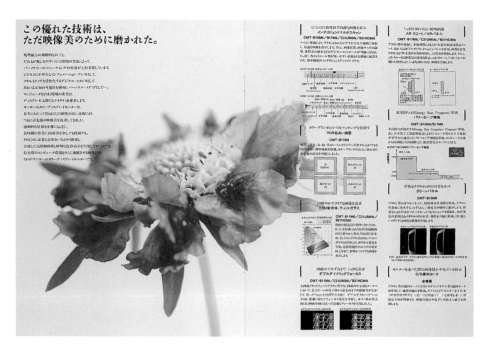

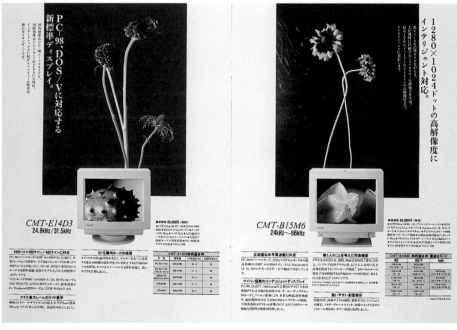

- **SANYO ELECTRIC CO., LTD.**

三洋電機㈱

Electrical equipment manufacturer /
電気製品メーカー

Product catalogue / 製品案内

1995

A: Hoso Syuppan Co., Ltd.　㈱放送出版

CD, AD: Ryoichi Yamakawa　山川亮一

D: Hirotaka Yamamoto　山本浩隆

P: Hisashi Murase　村瀬　永

CW: Shinya Kamimura　上村慎也

size: 297×210 mm

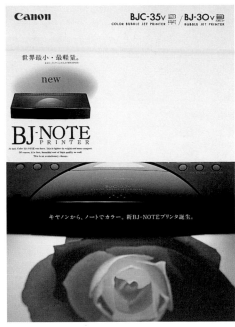

CANON SALES INC. •

キヤノン販売㈱

Precision equipment distributor /

精密機器販売

Product catalogue / 製品案内

1995

CD: Shinichi Enami　榎並伸一

AD: Hiroshi Tashiro　田代浩史

D: Hideki Toda　戸田英毅

P: Hiroshi Yoshida（Beans）

吉田　宏（ビーンズ）

CW: Hideki Numai / Hiroyuki Takano

沼井秀樹 / 高野裕之

DF: Dentsu / Bau Advertising Office

㈱電通 / ㈲バウ広告事務所

size: 297×210 mm

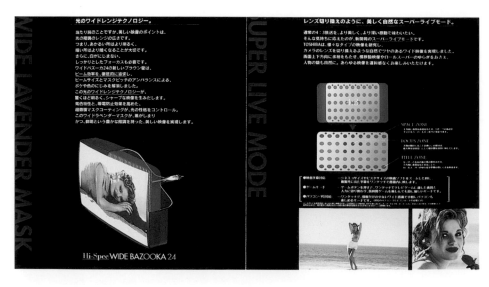

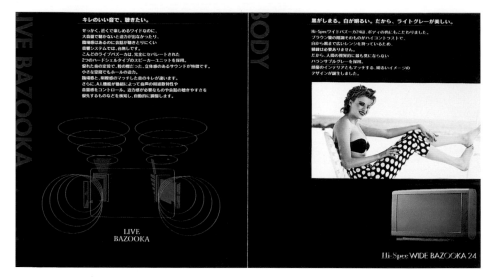

- **TOSHIBA CORPORATION**

　㈱東芝

Electrical equipment manufacturer /

電気製品メーカー

Product catalogue / 製品案内

1994

CD, AD: Osamu Moriya　森谷　統

D: Miki Tobita　飛田美紀

P: Naomi Kaltman

size: 200×180 mm

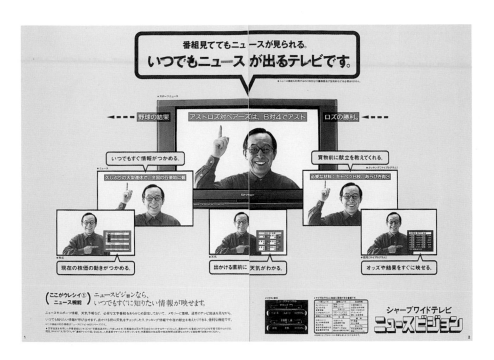

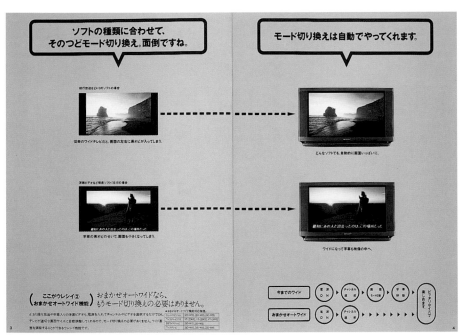

SHARP CORPORATION •

シャープ㈱

Electrical equipment manufacturer /

電気製品メーカー

Product catalogue / 製品案内

1994, 95

AD, D: Toppan Printing Co., Ltd.

Toppan Idea Center

凸版印刷㈱ トッパンアイディアセンター

P: Sharp Corporation Advertising Dept.

シャープ㈱ 宣伝部

size: 297×210 mm

Electrical Equipment • 161

ワンタッチな関係です。

もっと、ワンタッチ。新発売。

血中グルコース測定用
ワンタッチ®II

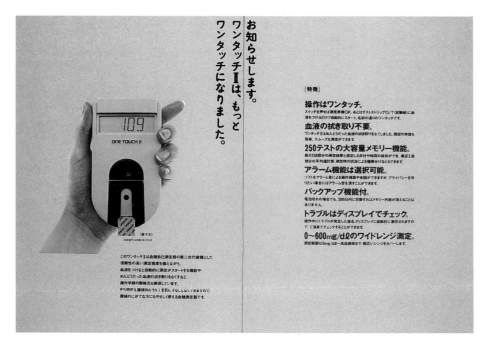

お知らせします。

ワンタッチIIは、もっと
ワンタッチになりました。

[特徴]

操作はワンタッチ。

血液の拭き取り不要。

250テストの大容量メモリー機能。

アラーム機能は選択可能。

バックアップ機能付。

トラブルはディスプレイでチェック。

0〜600mg/dℓのワイドレンジ測定。

血液感知で
オートスタート、
45秒で測定完了です。

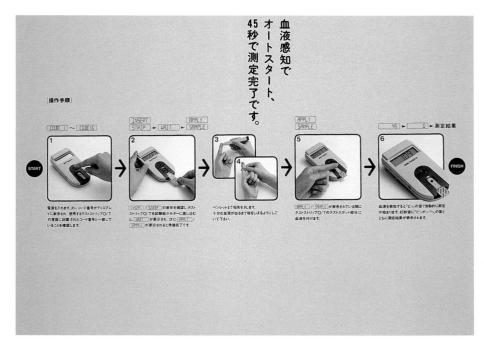

[操作手順]

いつもやさしい、
やわらかフォルムになりました。

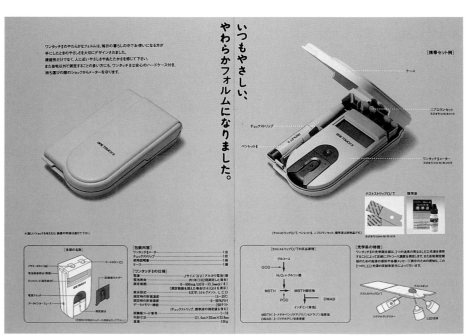

[携帯セット例]

• **EIKEN CHEMICAL CO., LTD.**

栄研化学㈱

Medical equipment manufacturer /
医療機器メーカー

Product catalogue / 製品案内

1992

CD, CW: Osamu Konashi　小梨　治

AD, D, I: Shuhei Yoshino　吉野修平

P: Eisho Watanabe　渡邊英昭

I: Nobuyuki Kuwahara　桑原伸之

DF: Yoshino Design Office

㈲ヨシノデザインオフィス

size: 297×210 mm

162 • **Electrical Equipment**

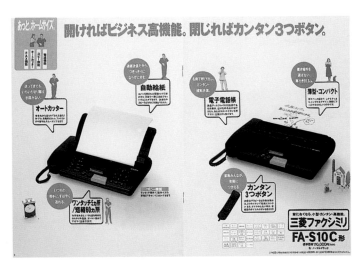

MITSUBISHI ELECTRIC •
CORPORATION

三菱電機㈱

Electrical equipment manufacturer /

電気製品メーカー

Product catalogue / 製品案内

1994

size: 297×210 mm

MITSUBISHI ELECTRIC •
CORPORATION

三菱電機㈱

Electrical equipment manufacturer /

電気製品メーカー

Product catalogue / 製品案内

1995

size: 297×210 mm

Electrical Equipment • 163

• SEIKO INSTRUMENTS INC.

セイコー電子工業㈱

Precision equipment manufacturer /
精密機器メーカー

Product catalogue / 製品案内

1992

AD, D: Hiroshi Yoshida　吉田 弘

P: Bungo Saito / Hisao Susuki

斉藤文護 / 薄　久夫

CW: Tomoji Taniguchi　谷口知二

DF: Creative Oricom

㈱クリエイティブ オリコム

size: 163×110 mm

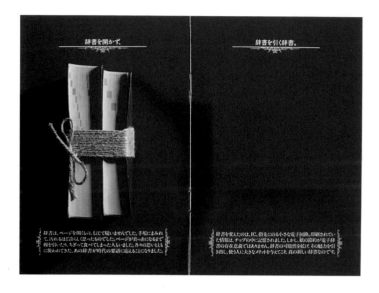

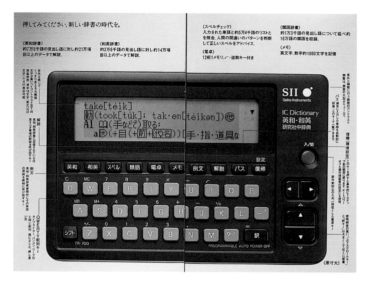

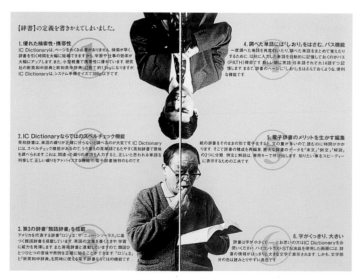

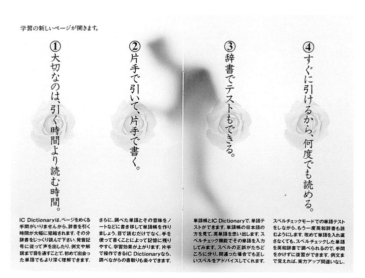

SEIKO INSTRUMENTS INC. •

セイコー電子工業㈱

Precision equipment manufacturer /

精密機器メーカー

Product catalogue / 製品案内

1993

AD, D: Hiroshi Yoshida　吉田 弘

P: Hisao Susuki　薄 久夫

CW: Tomoji Taniguchi　谷口知二

DF: Creative Oricom

㈱クリエイティブ オリコム

size: 163×110 mm

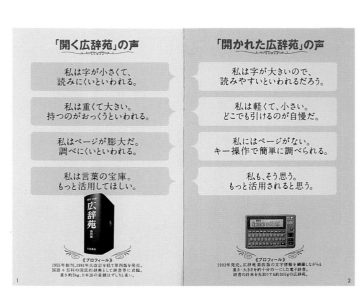

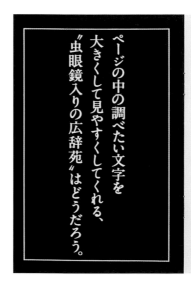

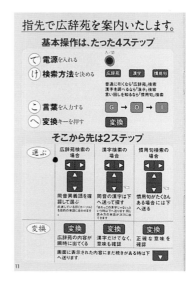

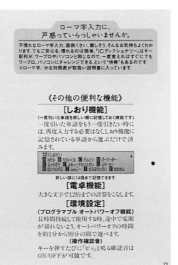

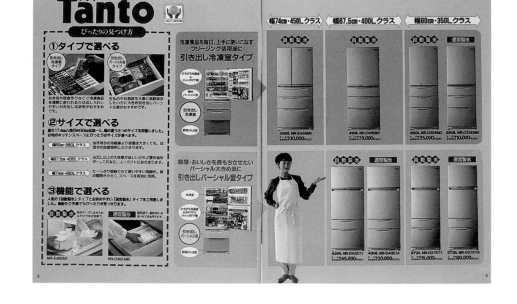

• **MATSUSHITA
REFRIGERATION COMPANY**

松下冷機㈱

Electrical equipment manufacturer /
電気製品メーカー

Product catalogue / 製品案内

1995

CD: Toshihiko Oka　岡　俊彦

AD: Nobuaki Onishi　大西庸晃

D: Suzuka Kuchiba / Naoki Takahashi
口羽涼香 / 高橋直木

P: Hisao Taira　平　寿夫

CW: Akiko Kunieda　国枝暁子

size: 297×210 mm

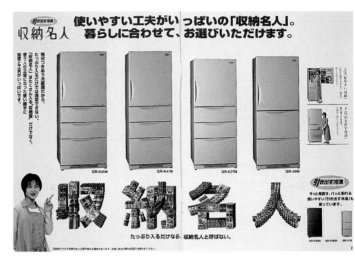

HITACHI, LTD. •

㈱日立製作所

Electrical equipment manufacturer /

電気製品メーカー

Product catalogue / 製品案内

1995

CD: Yukio Asami　浅見 由紀男

AD: Yasuharu Bansho　番匠泰治

D: Katsuhiko Ota　太田勝彦

P: Toshikazu Fujii　藤井利一

CW: Hiroyuki Kakinuma　柿沼裕之

DF: Senden Club　宣伝倶楽部

size: 297×210 mm

TOSHIBA CORPORATION •

㈱東芝

Electrical equipment manufacturer / 電気製品メーカー

Product catalogue / 製品案内

1995

CD, AD: Kitajima Masahiro　北島雅弘

D: Masanori Shimohara / Mieko Katsukura　下原正徳 / 勝倉 美栄子

P: Ura Kenichi / Yoshiharu Takahashi　浦 賢一 / 高橋芳晴

CW: Takaaki Saito / Nobuyuki Yamaguchi　斉藤孝明 / 山口信行

DF: Seed　㈱シード

size: 297×210 mm

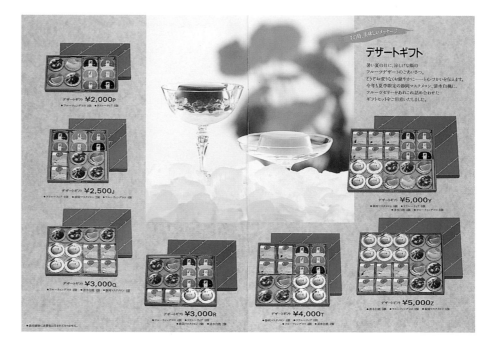

MUSK MELON & SHIMIZU HAKUTO
マスクメロン＆清水白桃

FRUITING COCO
フルーティングココ

GONCHAROFF CONFECTIONERY CO., LTD.

ゴンチャロフ製菓㈱

Confectionery maker / 洋菓子メーカー

Product catalogue / 製品案内

1995

CD, AD: Goncharoff
Confectionery Co., Ltd.

ゴンチャロフ製菓㈱ 企画部販売促進課

D: Atelier Aru / Ryosuke Makie

アトリエ・アール / 牧江良祐

CW: Sanae Kawata　川田早苗

size: 285×200 mm

LAFRUITEAR
ラフルーティア

CORBEILLE
コルベイユ

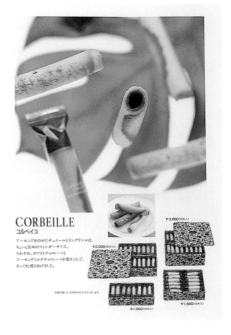

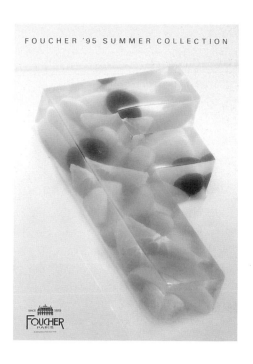

MATSUKAZEYA CO., LTD. •

㈱松風屋

Confectionery maker / 洋菓子メーカー

Product catalogue / 製品案内

1995

AD: Kenji Iwasaki　岩崎堅司

D: Yukiko Okabe　岡部 由紀子

P: Michihiro Tokuno　得能通弘

DF: Design Eye　㈱デザイン アイ

size: 297×210 mm

Food and drink • 169

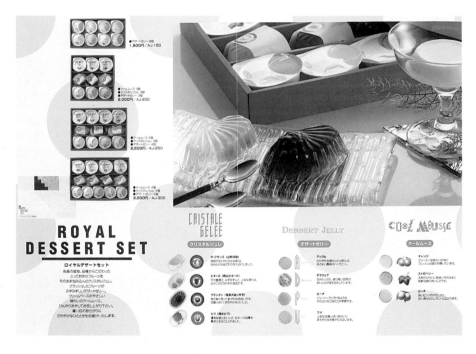

- **IZUMIYA CONFECTIONERY CO., LTD.**

㈱泉屋 東京店

Confectionery maker / 洋菓子メーカー

Product catalogue / 製品案内

1995

CD, AD: Meiho Syomoto　章本明平

D: Akio Syomoto　章本晃生

P: Masaharu Sakaue　坂上正治

DF: Studio. Orb Ltd.　㈲スタジオ．オオブ

size: 257×182 mm

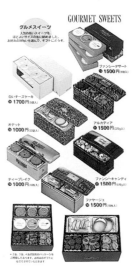

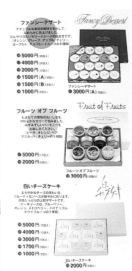

MOROZOFF LIMITED • 2

モロゾフ㈱

Confectionery maker / 洋菓子メーカー

Product catalogue / 製品案内

1995

CD: Keiko Miura　三浦啓子

CC: Megumi Fujimi　藤見　恵

AD: Kazuya Enomoto　榎本一弥

D: Yurika Nara　奈良百合香

P: Masashi Kudo　工藤正志

CW: Ryo Kusunoki　楠　涼

DF: Commercial Arts Institute

㈱商業美術研究所

size: 225×113 mm

ANTENOR CO., LTD. • 1

㈱アンテノール

Confectionery maker / 洋菓子メーカー

Product catalogue / 製品案内

1995

CD: Antenor Co., Ltd. Planning Dept.

㈱アンテノール 企画部

size: 257×175 mm

季節探しのティータイム

樹々には緑が、街には光が、新しい便りを運んで来ます。そよ風を
移ろう季節の一瞬を、しっかりとつかまえて、ゆったり味わうひと

テーブルに招いて、ティータイムにしませんか。
ときから、今日も一日がはじまります。

• **YOKU MOKU CO., LTD.**

㈱ヨックモック

Confectionery maker / 洋菓子メーカー

Product catalogue / 製品案内

1995

AD, D: Yukiyo Omori（Banquet）

大森幸代（ヴァンケット）

P: Masayuki Owa 大輪眞之

CW: Yoshiho Inoue 井上佳芳

S: Kazuyuki Taki 滝 和幸

size: 225×105 mm

KOBE DESSERT ISLAND • 2

神戸デザートアイランド

Confectionery maker / 洋菓子メーカー

Product catalogue / 製品案内

1994

CD, CW: Nobuo Kawakami　河上伸男

AD: Kazuaki Okazaki　岡崎和昭

D: Masami Otsuki　大槻昌美

P: Yoshinari Umemoto　梅本吉成

CW: Naoko Yasuda　安田直子

DF: Even Co., Ltd.

広告の仕事制作所　イーブン㈲

size: 210×148 mm

CONFECTIONERY KOTOBUKI • 1

㈱コンフェクショナリー コトブキ

Confectionery maker / 洋菓子メーカー

Product catalogue / 製品案内

1994

CD, CW: Nobuo Kawakami　河上伸男

AD: Kazuaki Okazaki　岡崎和昭

D: Masami Otsuki　大槻昌美

P: Yoshinari Umemoto　梅本吉成

CW: Naoko Yasuda　安田直子

DF: Even Co., Ltd.

広告の仕事制作所　イーブン㈲

size: 225×180 mm

京菓匠 鶴屋吉信

百菓涼覧

平成七年 夏号

銘菓

氷梅
こおりうめ

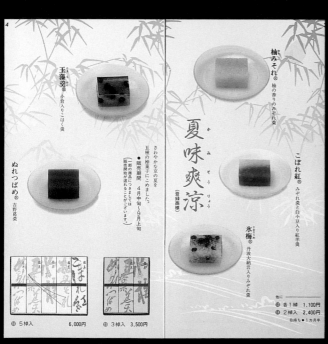

4

柚みぞれ㊞
柚の香りのみぞれ羹

玉藻㊞
小倉入りこはく羹

夏味爽涼
（登録商標）

こぼれ紅㊞
みぞれ羹と白小豆入り紅羊羹

ぬれつばめ㊞
吉野葛羹

さわやかな京の夏を
五種の棹菓子にこめました。

●販売期間
4月中旬〜9月上旬

氷梅㊞
こおりうめ
丹波大納言入りみぞれ羹

●一部の商品につきましては
（販売開始が遅れることがございます。）

他に
⑬ 各1棹　1,100円
⑭ 2棹入　2,400円

日持ち ●1カ月半

⑮ 5棹入　　6,000円
⑯ 3棹入　3,500円

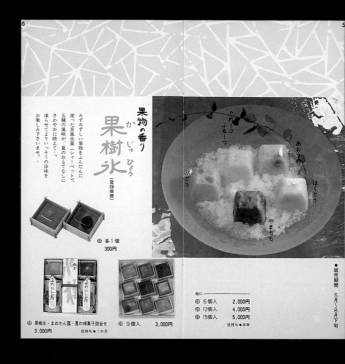

6

果物の香り
果樹氷
かじゅひょう
（登録商標）

みずみずしい果物をふんだんに
使った京風氷菓（シャーベット）。
五種の風味が、夏のおもてなしに
さわやかに映えて。
凍らせてよりいっそうの涼味を
お楽しみ下さいませ。

⑰ 各1個
300円

⑰ 果樹氷・まめかん寛・夏の棹菓子詰合せ
3,000円

⑱ 6個入　　2,000円
⑲ 12個入　4,000円
⑳ 15個入　5,000円

日持ち ●半年

⑱ 9個入　3,000円

●販売期間
5月〜8月下旬

日持ち ●1カ月

5

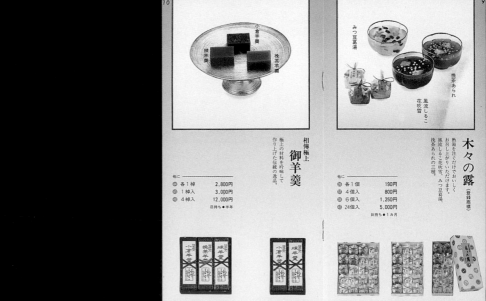

10

小倉芋羹

抹茶芋羹

練羊羹

相傳極上
御羊羹

極上の材料を吟味し
作り上げた伝統の逸品。

他に
⑬ 各1棹　2,800円
⑭ 1棹入　3,000円
⑮ 4棹入　12,000円

日持ち ●半年

⑯ 3棹入　9,000円
⑰ 2棹入　6,000円

みつ豆葛湯

風流しるこ
花吹雪

抹茶あられ

木々の露
（登録商標）

熱湯を注ぐだけでおいしく
お召し上がりいただけます。
風流しるこ花吹雪、みつ豆葛湯、
抹茶あられの三種。

他に
⑱ 各1個　190円
⑲ 4個入　800円
⑳ 6個入　1,250円
㉑ 24個入　5,000円

日持ち ●1カ月

⑱ 20個入　4,000円　⑲ 15個入　3,000円　⑳ 10個入　2,000円

9

TSURUYA YOSHINOBU

鶴屋吉信

Japanese confectionery maker /

和菓子メーカー

Product catalogue / 製品案内

1995

D: Tsuruya Yoshinobu

Business Planning Departme

鶴屋吉信 企画室

size: 210×105 mm

Food and Drink

しおり

赤坂 雪華堂

創業百年、ひたすらに
お茶のひととき、語らいの時、
食後の一服、お菓子は人と人と
の心をつなぎ、和をひろげ、寛
ろぎを与えてくれます。当堂は
徳川公より「雪の華のようだ」
とお賞めをいただきました金平
糖に始まり、時を経て、みぞれ
のようにしっとりした風合いの

甘納豆の製法を開発し、ひたす
ら豆の持ち味を活かしきること
に心を注いでまいりました。
先人の築いた基礎に、あせらず
吟味して、ひとつひとつ「味」を
積み上げてまいります菓子職人
としての喜びと誇りを、日々の
歩みとできます幸せに感謝いた
しております。

当主敬白

1

2

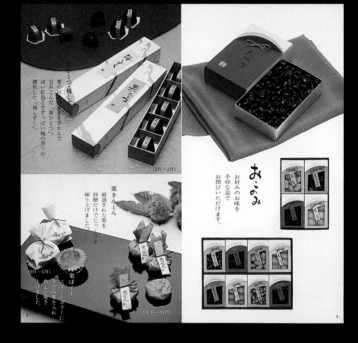

ひとつひとつ梅しずく
栗のお〜まるを芋かんで
包みこんだ「栗とつ」、
淡い紅色と甘ずっぱい梅の香りが
調和した「梅しずく」。

（9月〜3月）

おこのみ
お好みのお味を
手帳な量で
お撰びいただけます。

栗きんとん
厳選された栗を
砂糖だけでじっくりと
練り上げました。

栗ぼっと
スイートポテトに
さらさを入れ
他より抜き
上げました

（9月〜5月）

（9月〜11月）

6

5

水苑
うめ、いちご、あんずを
澄んだゼリーで
包みました。

星彩
梅ゆずぶどう
大納言を洋酒で
香りづけしたゼリーで包みました。

（4月〜8月）

水よう
こしゆず、ほうじ
涼やかな甘さが
ほんのり広がる

（5月〜8月）

（5月〜8月）

夏 旬の味 冬

栗きんとん

ゆたかに

丹波の黒豆を
ていねいに炊き上げた
「ゆたかに」

新たな年の餝りに
彩りそえる
「栗きんとん」

（11月〜1月）

7

SEKKADO

(有)雪華堂

Japanese confectionery maker /

和菓子メーカー

Product catalogue / 製品案内

1994

D: Yukie Hirayama　平山幸江

P: Echo Studio　エコースタジオ

size: 205×100 mm

Food and Drink

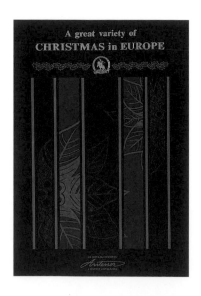

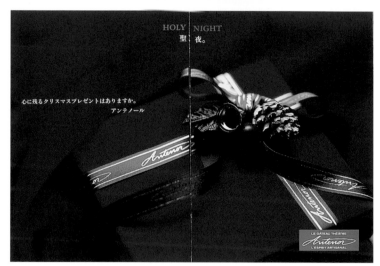

- **ANTENOR CO., LTD.**

㈱アンテノール

Confectionery maker / 洋菓子メーカー

Product catalogue / 製品案内

1994

CD: Antenor Co., Ltd. Planning Dept

㈱アンテノール 企画部

size: 210×150 mm

AKASAKA KAKIYAMA • CORPORATION

㈱赤坂柿山

Japanese confectionery makor /
和菓子メーカー

Product catalogue / 製品案内

1992

CD, D: Kizo Satake　佐竹起造

P: Hiroshi Nagaoka　長岡　宏

CW: Hisako Ogino　荻野寿子

S: Hideo Saito　斉藤秀夫

DF: Satake Kizo Design Office
佐竹起造デザイン事務所

size: 110×220 mm

ANTENOR CO., LTD. •

㈱アンテノール

Confectionery maker / 洋菓子メーカー

Product catalogue / 製品案内

1995

CD: Antenor Co., Ltd. Planning Dept.

㈱アンテノール 企画部

size: 200×110 mm

—Beppe Spadacini Linea Casa

*There used to be a special place
like a garden Adam & Eve lived*

Feel the wind, Feel yourself.

- **NISHIKAWA SANGYO CO., LTD.**
西川産業㈱

Bedding, furniture manufacturer /
寝具・家具メーカー

Product catalogue / 製品案内

1992

AD, D: Katsunori Hironaka　弘中克典

CW: Atsushi Miyao　宮尾　惇

P: Juro Hayashi　林　十郎

size: 297×220 mm

Sleep like an angel.

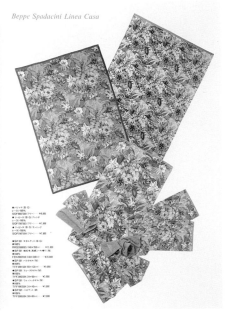

Beppe Spadacini Linea Casa

●パッケB·G·
レース100%
SOF98726·(フラワー)……　¥5,680
●ショール B·G·アッシュ
レース100%
SOF19038×(グリーン)…¥7,680
●ショールB·G·テュニック
レース100%
SOF98768X(フラワー)…¥7,880

●SP131 タオルケット B·G·
綿100%
RKS35885×146×70×……　¥12,680
●SP131 綿毛布(本綿ニット)B·G·(M)
綿100%
SP135W35893×180×210×…¥15,680
●SP131 バスタオル B·G·
綿100%
TFF20135X(58×125×)…¥5,880
●SP131 フェースタオル(M)
綿100%
TFF29023X(34×84×)…¥3,980
●SP131 ウォッシュタオル B·G·
綿100%
TFF98735X(34×43×)…¥1,380
●SP131 バスマット(M)
綿100%
TFF72985X(58×85×)…¥2,880

Beppe Spadacini Linea Casa

●SP120 花もようとらS(GR·G)
表地　綿100%
中わた　ポリエステル(ANIMEEREN)1.3㎏
松和RS56013(169×210×)…¥188,680
●SP131 タオルケットS(GR·G)
表地　綿100%
中わた　ポリウレタン85%·綿%
KLW35803(169×210×)…¥39,000
●SP131 毛布(綿毛ふとんLS(GR·G)
表地　綿100%
中わた　ウール90%·PC85%·毛リPE·セミロ×
KGW32045(169×210×)…¥39,000
●SP131 お軽量ふとんS(GR·G)
表地　綿100%
中わた　ウール85%·PE85%·毛リ×ボ×·綿S·Ao×
KCW34015(169×210×)…¥39,000
●SP131 敷きばとん(GR·G)
表地　綿100%
中わた　フェザー%
KKW35013(169×210×)…¥39,000

●SP131 花もようとんdAB(GR·G)
表地　綿100%
中わた　ポリテテン(ANIMEX85%)1.0㎏
KLW35035(169×210×)…¥159,680
●SP131 タオルケットd(GR·G)
表地　綿100%
中わた　ポリウレタン·綿%
KLW35825(169×210×)…¥43,000
●SP131 毛布(綿毛ふとんLS(GR·G)
表地　綿100%
中わた　ウール90%·PE85%·毛リ×·セミ·90×·マ·b×
KXW44007(169×210×)…¥39,380
●SP131 お軽量ふとん(GR·G)
表地　綿100%
中わた　フェザー95%
KKW35013(169×210×)…¥39,380
●ミホールセット…¥275,680

●SP131 枕よ2カバー S·B·G·
綿100%
PT18074S(169×39×)…¥4,580
●SP131 枕よ2カバー(M)
綿100%
PT18074S(169×39×)…¥7,680
●SP131 ピローケース B·G·
綿100%
PT14064S(52×93×)…¥3,180
●SP131 枕よ2カバーSL B·G·
綿100%
PT18083S(169×210×)…¥5,280
●SP131 枕よ2カバーSL B·G·
綿100%
PT18083S(169×210×)…¥5,280
●SP131 枕よ2カバーSL B·G·
綿100%
全上掛　169×210×…¥12,680
●SP131 枕よ2カバーDL B·G·
綿100%
全上掛　169×210×…¥4,680

●SP131 コンフォーターケースSL(M)
表地·裏地綿100%
CTPi35035(169×139×)…¥39,680
●SP131 コンフォーターケースSL(M)
表地·裏地綿100%
CTF40305(169×139×)…¥33,680
●SP131 コンフォーターケースDL(M)
表地·裏地綿100%
CTFi35035(169×210×)…¥74,000
●SP131 コンフォーターケースDL(M)
表地·裏地綿100%
CTF35035(169×210×)…¥39,000
●SP131 ピローケース(M)
表地·裏地綿100%
CTFi35015(58×39×)…¥27,680
●SP131 ピローケース(M)
表地·裏地綿100%
CSFi35035(30×58×)…¥1,180
●SP131 ピローシーC·B·G·
表地　綿50%·クリ×ステ×50%
CFFi33915(225×210×)…¥5,580
●SP131 エプロン(M)
表地　綿50%·クリ×ステ×50%
CFFi35035(30×58×)…¥3,880
…バイオレーン·SP131·89本FT×50·

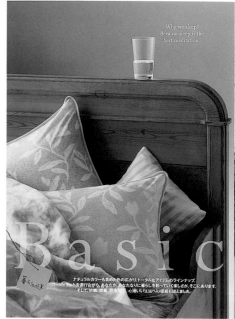

COVERING TOTAL

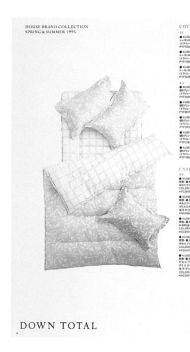

DOWN TOTAL

TOWELKET & BLANKET

• **NISHIKAWA SANGYO CO., LTD.**

西川産業㈱

Bedding, furniture manufacturer /

寝具・家具メーカー

Product catalogue / 製品案内

1995

AD, D: Katsunori Hironaka　弘中克典

P: Noboru Morikawa　森川　昇

CW: Atsushi Miyao　宮尾　惇

S: Midori Araki　荒木　みどり

size: 297×210 mm

180 • Home

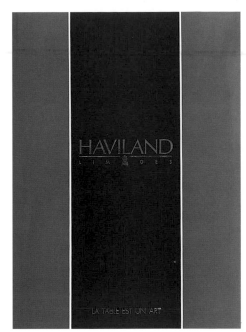

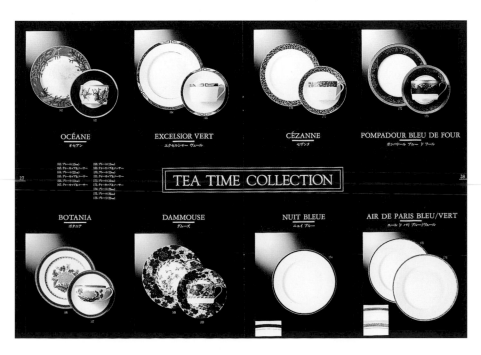

DE LA COLLECTION •

デラ コレクション

Trading company / 貿易業

Product catalogue / 製品案内

1994

CD: Yoshikazu Tanikawa　谷河義和

AD, D: Hidenori Okahashi　岡橋秀則

P: Kenji Miyazaki　宮崎賢次

CW: Kaoru Yamashita　山下　薫

DF: Lotoath Design Studio

ロトアス デザイン スタジオ

size: 297×210 mm

- **ACTUS CO., LTD.**

　㈱アクタス

Furniture importer / 家具輸入販売

Product catalogue / 製品案内

1995

CD, D, S: Masanori Araki（Actus）

　荒木正則（アクタス）

AD: Toru Oshige（Actus）

　大重 亨（アクタス）

P: Keiji Ishiuchi / Yoshikazu Watase

　石内敬二 / 渡瀬良和

CW: Yuko Ito（Actus）　伊東裕子（アクタス）

S: Michiko Kobayashi　小林 みちこ

size: 297×210 mm

Church 831120
W 390 D 490 H 812 SH 430 ¥34,000
メープル／ライトブラウン ステイン塗りオイル仕上げ

Chair

Chair

Bring [ランドリーチェアー] 662304 ¥15,000　Varnes [ランドリーボックス] 967302 ¥7,800

Double Line-C 991104
W 750 D 660 H 1,800 ¥183,000
カバ／ミディアムブラウン ステイン塗りクリア塗装

Double Line-B 991107
W 430 D 660 H 1,800 ¥180,000
カバ／ミディアムブラウン ステイン塗りクリア塗装

Double Line-A 991106
W 1,000 D 660 H 830 ¥165,000
カバ／ミディアムブラウン ステイン塗りクリア塗装

Wardrobe Cabinet Chest

Wardrobe Cabinet Chest

Oslo [チェアー] 831138 ¥35,000

Stick 831140
Ø 1,100 H 740 ¥90,000
突板［オーク／ライトブラウン ステイン塗りクリア塗装
脚［ビーチ／ミディアムブラウン ステイン塗りクリア塗装］
仕様：ノックダウン［組み立て式］

Select 831142
W 1,800 H 800 D 900 H 740 ¥160,000
カバ／ミディアムブラウン ステイン塗りクリア塗装

Horn Round 831145
メープル／ライトオフホワイト ステイン塗りクリア塗装

Horn 831141
W 1,500 D 750 H 760 ¥150,000
メープル／ライトブラウン ステイン塗りクリア塗装

Slender Straight Leg 1500 831139
W 1,500 D 750 H 720 ¥130,000
カバ／ミディアムブラウン ステイン塗りクリア塗装
仕様：ノックダウン［組み立て式］

Slender Straight Leg 900 831136
W 900 D 900 H 720 ¥90,000
カバ／ミディアムブラウン ステイン塗りクリア塗装
仕様：ノックダウン［組み立て式］

Slender Curve Leg 1500 831137
W 1,500 D 750 H 720 ¥130,000
カバ／ミディアムブラウン ステイン塗りクリア塗装
仕様：ノックダウン［組み立て式］

Slender Curve Leg 900 831138
W 900 D 900 H 720 ¥90,000
カバ／ミディアムブラウン ステイン塗りクリア塗装
仕様：ノックダウン［組み立て式］

Table

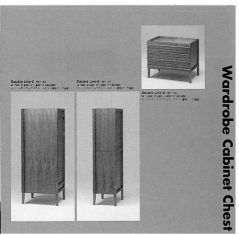

Table

SAZABY •

㈱サザビー

Home accessories supplier /

家具・アクセサリー・雑貨等輸入製造販売

Product catalogue / 製品案内

1994

AD, DF: Sazaby Graphic Design

サザビー グラフィックデザイン

D: Hatsuko Kobayashi / Chie Kusakari

小林初子 / 草刈千絵

P: Takahiro Kurokawa /

IMA/Urbane Inc.

黒川隆広 / ㈱イマ/アーバン

size: 210×210 mm

Home • 183

テーブル＆チェア
'94-5
AROUND
THE BIG TABLE

Around
Big Table

目常を、心ゆたかに積みかさねるために。

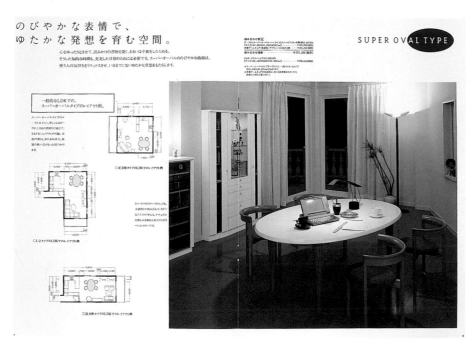

SUPER OVAL TYPE

のびやかな表情で、
ゆたかな発想を育む空間。

人のこだわりと、
先端技術の出会い。
そこからビクターの品質が
誕生します。

• **VICTOR COMPANY OF
JAPAN, LIMITED**

日本ビクター㈱ インテリア事業部

Furniture supplier / 家具製造販売

Product catalogue / 製品案内

1994

CD: Shinji Miyagaki　宮垣真二

AD: Yasuaki Handa　半田泰明

D: Tamotsu Shimada

嶋田 保（嶋田デザイン事務所）

P: Yoshihiko Kuwata（Knack）

桑田義彦（Knack）

CW: Shinya Kamimura　上村慎也

S: Seiji Sageshima /

Shintaro Sakagami

下嶋世司 / 坂上 信太郎（下嶋事務所）

DF: Monolith, Inc.　㈱モノリス

size: 297×210 mm

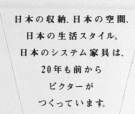

日本の収納、日本の空間、
日本の生活スタイル。
日本のシステム家具は、
20年も前から
ビクターが
つくっています。

自在に組み合わせることで、
住まう人の個性を表現する。
エクステが創る
「暮らし方」をご紹介します。

例えば、種類や形が全く違う
たくさんの食器を隠すのではなく、
美しく見せるという発想。

VICTOR COMPANY •
OF JAPAN, LIMITED

日本ビクター㈱インテリア事業部

Furniture supplier / 家具製造販売
Product catalogue / 製品案内
1994
CD: Shinji Miyagaki　宮垣真二
AD, D: Yasuaki Handa　半田泰明
D: Tamotsu Shimada
嶋田　保（嶋田デザイン事務所）
P: Makoto Kubo (Knack)
久保　誠（Knack）
CW: Ryuichi Masuda　増田隆一
S: Haruko Ishimasa / Sachiko Omi /
Tomoko Miyawaki (Knack)
石政春子 / 大見 佐知子 / 宮脇知子（Knack）
DF: Monolith, Inc.　㈱モノリス
size: 297×210 mm

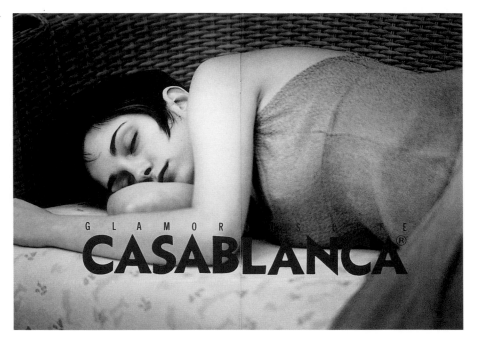

• **MURATA GODO INC.**

㈱村田合同

Furniture maker / 家具メーカー

Product catalogue / 製品案内

1995

size: 364×257 mm

La vista ラビスタ アームチェア¥11,000（にファブリック）

Hortus ホルタス アームチェア¥43,000／ホルタス テーブル¥95,000／ホルタス サイドテーブル¥47,500

PINO
COLLEZIONE

1

CERTO

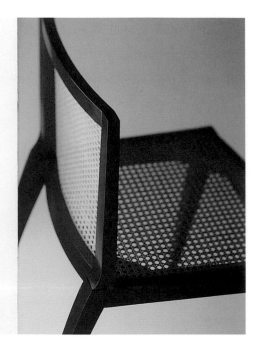

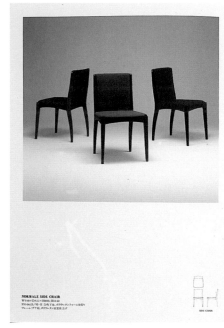

NORMALE SIDE CHAIR

NORMALE ARM CHAIR

FILO

- **PINO CORPORATION**
  ピノ コーポレーション

  Furniture maker / 家具メーカー
  Product catalogue / 製品案内
  1994
  AD, D: Hitoshi Babasaki　馬場崎 仁
  P: Mars　マルス
  size: 297×210 mm

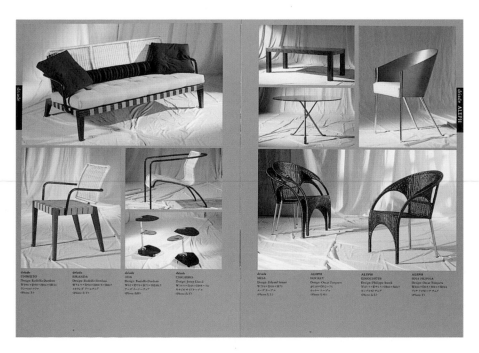

**AMBIENTE •
INTERNATIONAL INC.**

㈱アンビエンテ・インターナショナル

Furniture importer / 家具輸入販売

Product catalogue / 製品案内

1994

D: Hidetoshi Mito　美登英利

DF: Mitográfico　ミトグラフィコ

size: 297×210 mm

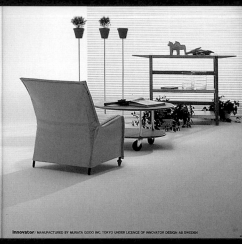

innovator/ MANUFACTURED BY MURATA GODO INC. TOKYO UNDER LICENCE OF INNOVATOR DESIGN AB SWEDEN

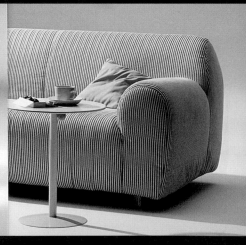

»boom«
ブーム／ソファ

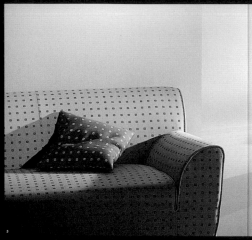

• **MURATA GODO INC.**
㈱村田合同

Furniture maker / 家具メーカー
Product catalogue / 製品案内
1995
size: 200×210 mm

STUDIO·LINE ®
STUDIO LINE INTERNATIONAL COLLECTION/MANUFACTURED AND DISTRIBUTED BY MURATA GODO INC. TOKYO

'95

Tea
ティー
MADE IN ITALY Design: Edy Ciani
¥36,000
シート／グリーン
フレーム／ブナ材ウレタン塗装／ブラウン

Tonda
トンダ
MADE IN ITALY Design: Edy Ciani
¥34,000
シート／グリーン
フレーム／ブナ材ウレタン塗装／ブラウン

3

4

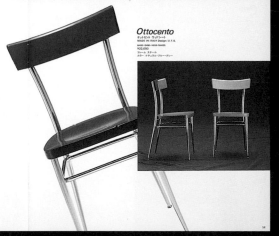

Ottocento
オットセント レザーシート
MADE IN ITALY Design: U.T.S.
¥29,000
シート／レザー（合成皮）
フレーム／スチール
カラー／ベージュ・グリーン

Ottocento
オットセント ウッドシート
MADE IN ITALY Design: U.T.S.
¥22,000
フレーム／スチール
カラー／ナチュラル・ブルー・グレー

13

14

Olivier Villatte
オリビエ・ルビラーテ
MADE IN FRANCE Design: Olivier Villatte

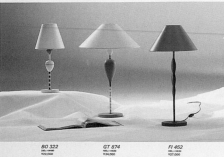

※すべて ビ・ピーカー＆ A-5E11

BO 322	GT 874	FI 452	ND 122	1035 B	1035 U	JM 910
¥22,000	¥34,000	¥27,000	¥49,000	¥49,000	¥48,000	¥49,000

27

28

MURATA GODO INC. •
㈱村田合同

Furniture maker / 家具メーカー
Product catalogue / 製品案内
1995
size: 200×210 mm

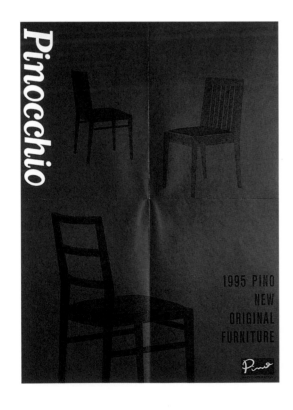

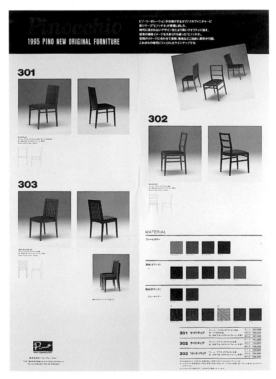

- **PINO CORPORATION**

ピノ コーポレーション

Furniture maker / 家具メーカー
Product catalogue / 製品案内
1994
AD, D: Hitoshi Babasaki　馬場崎 仁
P: Mars　マルス
size: 297×210 mm

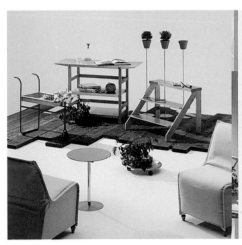

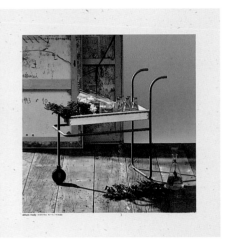

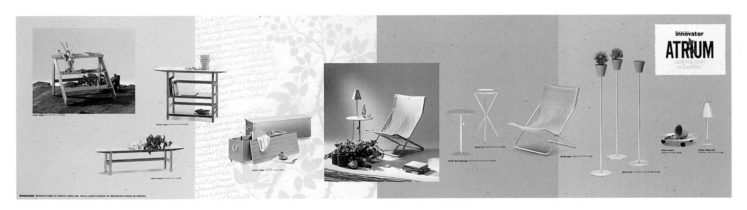

MURATA GODO INC. •

㈱村田合同

Furniture maker / 家具メーカー

Product catalogue / 製品案内

1995

size: 255×255 mm

Home • 193

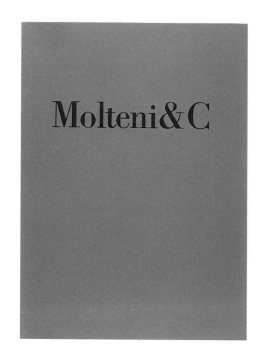

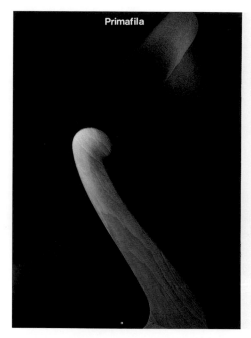

Primafila

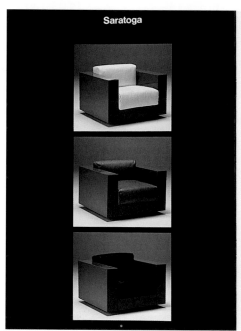

Saratoga

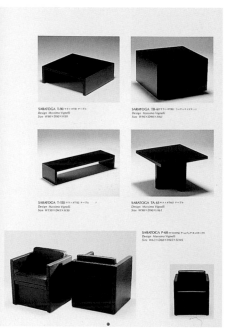

- **AMBIENTE
INTERNATIONAL INC.**

㈱アンビエンテ・インターナショナル

Furniture importer / 家具輸入販売

Product catalogue / 製品案内

1992

AD: Fumikazu Sakuraba　桜庭文一

P: Kenji Niiyama　新山健次

DF: CIEL　㈲シエル

size: 297×210 mm

No Stop

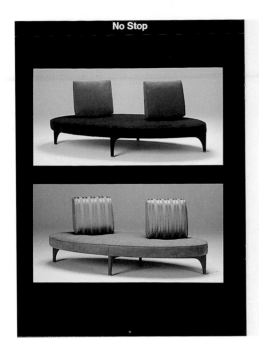

NO STOP／ノーストップ イージーソファ
Design Maarten Kusters
Size W252×D112×H90×SH37

Ronda

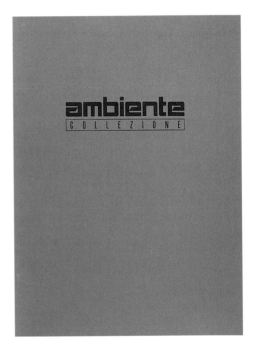

RONDA 710／ロンダ アームチェア
Design Afra & Tobia Scarpa
Size W79×D64×H82×SH44

RONDA 710-S／ロンダ アームチェア（キャスター付）
Afra & Tobia Scarpa
Size W79×D64×H84×SH43

Aida

AIDA／アイーダ アームチェア
Design Giorgio Ragazzini
Size W49×D43×H82×SH46

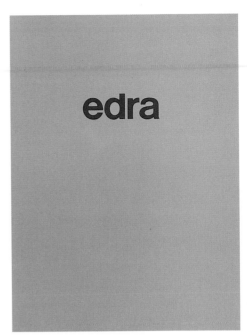

edra

ambiente
COLLEZIONE

mazzei

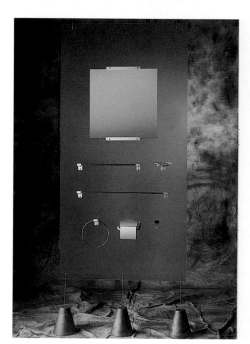

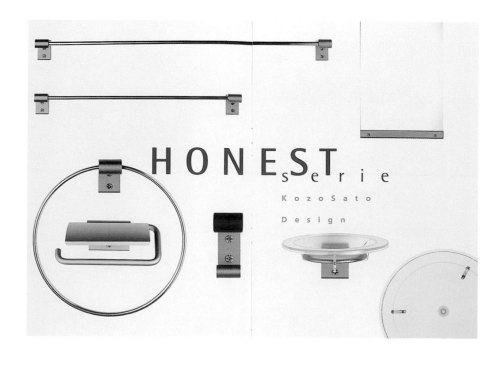

- **INTERFORM MFG. INC.**

㈱インターフォーム エムエフジー

Building accessories manufacturer /
建築金物メーカー

Product catalogue / 製品案内

1995

AD, D: Jun Sato　佐藤　淳

P: Joe Sugino　杉野　譲

CW: Kozo Sato　佐藤康三

DF: Jun Sato Design Inc.

佐藤　淳 デザイン室

size: 297×210 mm

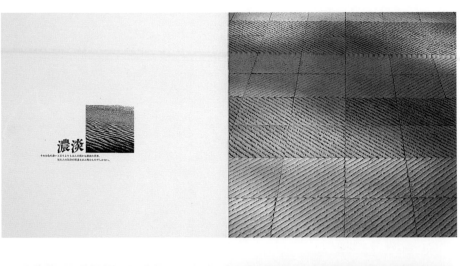

NIHON KOGYO CO., LTD. •

日本興業㈱

Construction components

manufacturer / 建築部材メーカー

Product catalogue / 製品案内

1995

AD: Koichi Sato　佐藤晃一

P: Ken Yamauchi　山内　健

size: 235×240 mm

Construction •

- **UPLINK CO.**
㈲アップリンク

Movie distributor / 映画配給
Product catalogue, movie brochure /
製品案内・映画パンフレット
1990
CD: Takashi Asai 浅井 隆
AD, D: Atsushi Ebina 海老名 淳
size: 125×145 mm

UPLINK CO. •

㈲アップリンク

Movie distributor / 映画配給
Movie brochure / 映画パンフレット
1995
CD: Takashi Asai　浅井　隆
AD, D: Atsushi Ebina　海老名 淳
size: 225×155 mm

Music and Media • 199

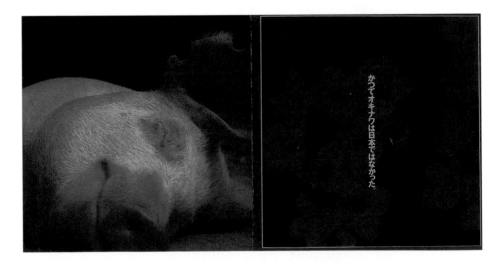

- **PARCO CO., LTD.**

  ㈱パルコ

  Entertainment production / イベント企画
  Movie brochure / 映画パンフレット
  1989
  CD: Natsuki Haryu　針生夏樹
  AD, D, I: Atsushi Ebina　海老名 淳
  P: Masashi Kuwamoto　桑本正士
  size: 210×210 mm

PARCO CO., LTD. •

㈱パルコ

Entertainment production / イベント企画
Movie brochure / 映画パンフレット
1994
CD: Manabu Kaneko　金子　学
AD, D: Atsushi Ebina　海老名　淳
P: Masashi Kuwamoto　桑本正士
size: 265×190 mm

Music and Media • 201

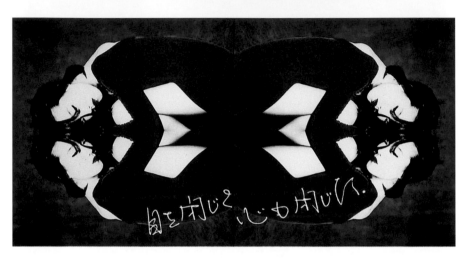

• **PARCO CO., LTD.**

㈱パルコ

Entertainment production / イベント企画
Concert program / コンサート パンフレット
1994
AD, D: Atsushi Ebina 海老名 淳
P: Seishi Takamiya （Cover） /
Akihito Kubota
高宮青志（表紙）/ 久保田 昭人
I, CW: Akina Nakamori 中森明菜
size: 210×210 mm

Either
Silence
or
Noise,

YUI MUSIC FACTORY •

ユイ音楽工房

Artist management / プロダクション

Concert program / コンサート パンフレット

1994

CD, AD: Osamu Moriya　森谷　統

D: Miki Tobita / Masako Iimori

飛田美紀 / 飯森雅子

P: Takeo Ogiso　小木曽 威夫

size: 370×265 mm

Music and Media •

- **B PROJECT INC.**
  ㈱ ビー プロジェクト

  Artist management / プロダクション
  Concert program / コンサート パンフレット
  1995
  AD: Ichiro Mitani　三谷一郎
  D: Yoko Nakamura　中村陽子
  P: Itaru Hirama　平間　至
  size: 360×255 mm

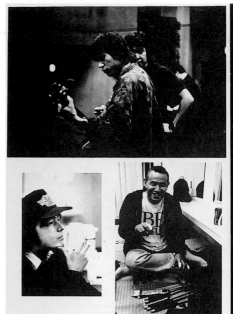

JUGGLER CO., LTD. / •
POP ROCK COMPANY
ジャグラー / ポップ ロック カンパニー
Artist management, souvenir retailer /
アーティスト マネージメント、
コンサートグッズ販売
Concert program / コンサート パンフレット
1994
AD, D, P: Takayuki Uchiyama　内山高之
P: Junichi Takahashi / Keiko Sasaki
高橋淳一 / 佐々木 ケイコ
size: 360×255 mm

Music and Media • 205

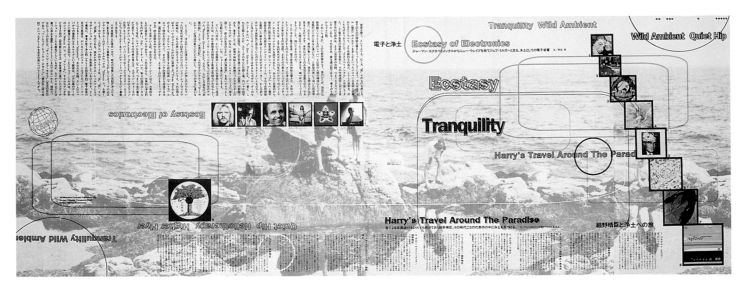

• **MERCURY MUSIC**
  ENTERTAINMENT CO., LTD.
マーキュリー ミュージック
エンタテインメント㈱

Music software manufacturer /
音楽ソフト製造
Product catalogue / 製品案内
1995
AD: Yasushi Fujimoto　藤本 やすし
D: Chikako Yamamoto　山本 知香子
size: 148×140 mm

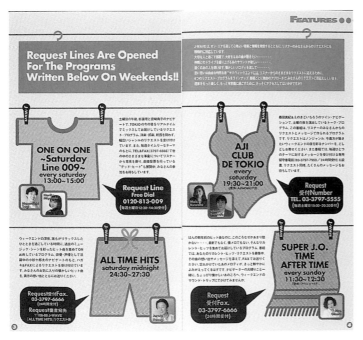

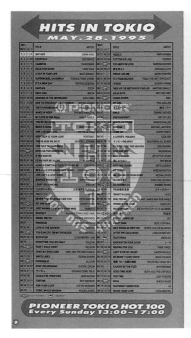

FM JAPAN (J-WAVE) •

㈱エフエム ジャパン（J-WAVE）

Radio station / 放送局

Program guide / 番組案内

1995

size: 257×140 mm

Music and Media • 207

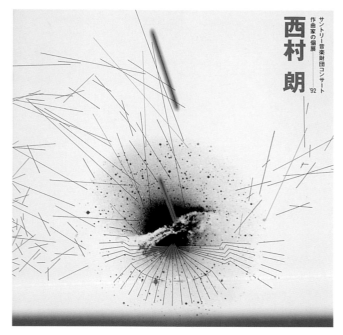

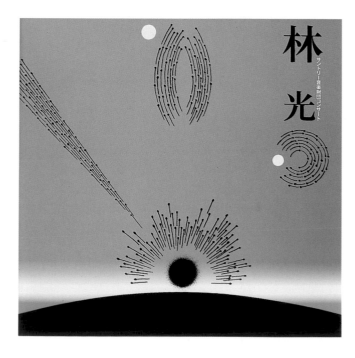

• **SUNTORY**
MUSIC FOUNDATION

(財)サントリー音楽財団

Music foundation / 音楽財団
Concert program / コンサート パンフレット
1991 - 95
D: Tokiyoshi Tsubouchi 坪内祝義
size: 250×250 mm

Josephine Komara

NHK SERVICE CENTER INC. ●
OSAKA BRANCH

㈶NHK サービスセンター 大阪支局

TV station service center /

テレビ局 サービスセンター

Exhibition guide / 展覧会パンフレット

1993

AD, D: Masaaki Hiromura　廣村正彰

D: Takafumi Kusagaya　草谷隆文

P: Masayuki Hayashi　林 雅之

DF: Hiromura Design Office, Inc.

㈱廣村デザイン事務所

size: 340×340 mm

鈴木五郎展
Suzuki Goro Exhibit
Thursday, October 21 –
Tuesday, October 26,1993
8th Floor Gallery Maruei Skyle

丸栄会社設立50周年記念 — 1993年10月21日[木] — 26日[火] — 丸栄スカイル8階画廊

● **GORO SUZUKI**

鈴木五郎

Ceramic artist / 陶芸作家

Exhibit guide / 個展パンフレット

1993

AD: Ichiro Mitani 三谷一郎

D: Yoko Nakamura 中村陽子

P: Gakuji Tanaka 田中学而

size: 297×215 mm

KAZUO TAKIGUCHI •

滝口和男

Ceramic artist / 陶芸作家
Exhibit guide / 個展パンフレット
1994
AD: Ichiro Mitani　三谷一郎
D: Yoko Nakamura　中村陽子
P: Gakuji Tanaka　田中学而
size: 297×210 mm

Events • 211

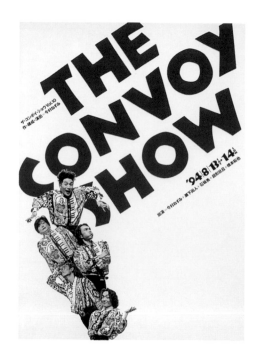

welcome!

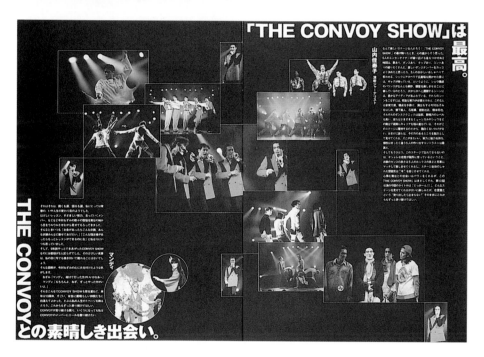

「THE CONVOY SHOW」は最高。

THE CONVOYとの素晴しき出会い。

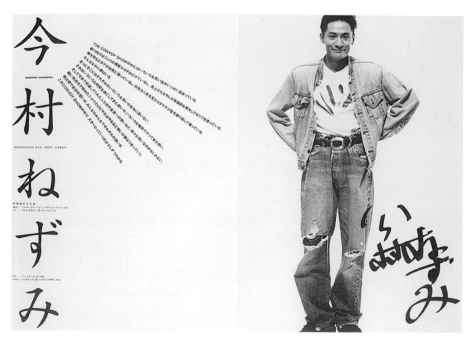

今村ねずみ

- **THE CONVOY**

ザ・コンボイ

Theater group / パフォーマンス グループ

Program / 公演パンフレット

1994

CD, AD, D: Shuhei Yoshino　吉野修平

D: Hisako Chatani　茶谷寿子

P: Eisho Watanabe　渡邊英昭

DF: Yoshino Design Office

㈲ヨシノデザインオフィス

size: 364×257 mm

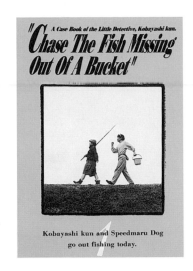

A Case Book of the Little Detective, Kobayashi kun.

"Chase The Fish Missing Out Of A Bucket"

Kobayashi kun and Speedmaru Dog go out fishing today.

1

2 "Hurray!! I get a big catch!!"

"Why, my fish have vanished!"

Now, a trouble happens.

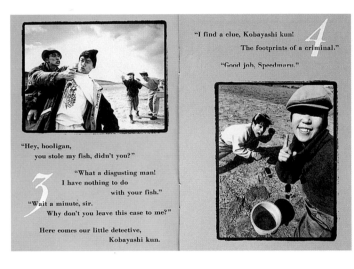

"Hey, hooligan,
you stole my fish, didn't you?"

"What a disgusting man!
I have nothing to do
with your fish."

3 "Wait a minute, sir.
Why don't you leave this case to me?"

Here comes our little detective,
Kobayashi kun.

"I find a clue, Kobayashi kun!
The footprints of a criminal." *4*

"Good job, Speedmaru."

"Because......Daddy, *6*
deep bodied bitterling
is a kind of
red data animals."

5 "Look! The criminal is setting fish
free overthere!"

"Oh, my God! That's my son!"

PLANET PISTACCIO •

惑星ピスタチオ

Theater company / 劇団

Program / 演劇パンフレット

1995

D: Takeshi Kuroda　黒田武志

P: Miwa Isoi　磯井美和

CW: Shatner Nishida　西田 シャトナー

DF: Office Sandscape

オフィス・サンドスケイプ

size: 148×105 mm

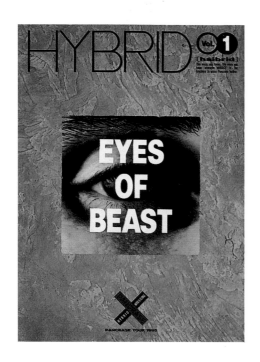

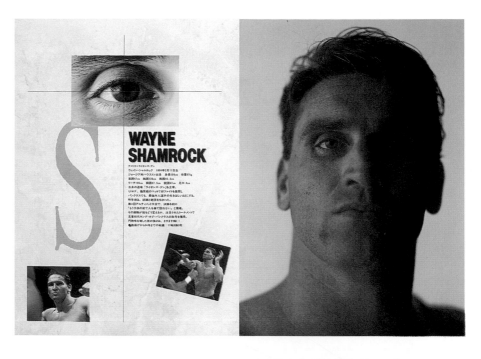

- **WORLD PANCRASE CREATE, INC.**

  ㈱ワールド パンクラス クリエイト

  Professional wrestling promoter /

  プロレス興業

  Wrestling program /

  プロレス興業 パンフレット

  1995

  AD: Michio Takano　高野道雄

  D: Eiji Okusa / Yasuyuki Uchima

  大草栄治 / 内間安幸

  P: Masahiro Hashimoto　橋本昌弘

  CW: Taku Nishida　西田 琢

  DF: ADD, Inc.　㈱ ADD

  size: 364×257 mm

いま、一度、宣言しよう。
進化するプロレス、
ハイブリッド・レスリング。

TRANSFIGHTING
Wayne Shamrock vs Bas Rutten

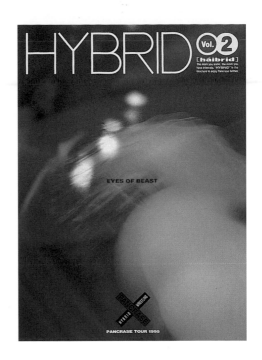

HYBRID Vol.2

[háibrid]
The more you know, the more you have interests, "HYBRID" is the brochure to enjoy Pancrase further.

EYES OF BEAST

PANCRASE TOUR 1995

Suzuki Minoru

Funaki Masakatsu

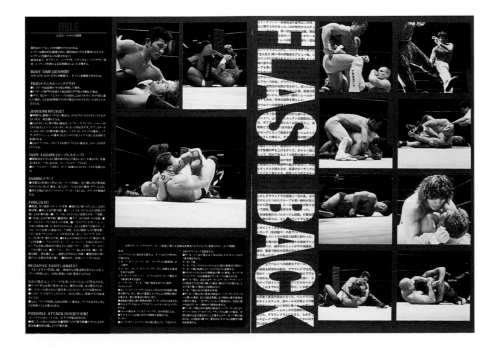

WORLD PANCRASE •
CREATE, INC.

㈱ワールド パンクラス クリエイト

Professional wrestling promoter /
　プロレス興業

Wrestling program /
　プロレス興業 パンフレット

1995

AD: Michio Takano 高野道雄

D: Eiji Okusa / Yasuyuki Uchima
　大草栄治 / 内間安幸

P: Masahiro Hashimoto 橋本昌弘

CW: Taku Nishida 西田 琢

DF: ADD, Inc. ㈱ ADD

size: 364×257 mm

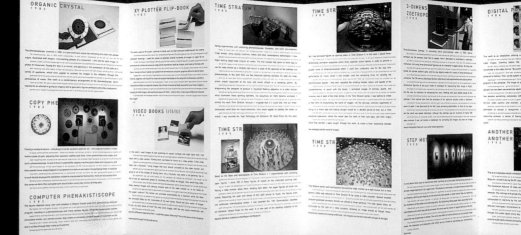

INDEX

SUBMITTOR INDEX

CLIENT INDEX

Jacket Design
Kyoko Nomura

Art Director / Designer
Miyuki Kawanabe

Editors
Etsuko Kitagami
Ayako Aoyama

Editorial Manager
Masato Ieshiro

Photographer
Kuniharu Fujimoto

Coordinator
Chizuko Gilmore (San Francisco)

English Translator / Consultant
Sue Herbert

Publisher
Shingo Miyoshi

カタログ & パンフレット コレクション
Catalog & Pamphlet Collection
vol.3

2003 年 1 月 8 日初版第 1 刷発行

発行所　ピエ・ブックス
〒 170-0003　東京都豊島区駒込 4-14-6　ビラフェニックス 301
編集 Tel: 03-3949-5010　Fax: 03-3949-5650
　e-mail: editor@piebooks.com
営業 Tel: 03-3940-8302　Fax: 03-3576-7361
　e-mail: sales@piebooks.com

2003 年 3 月 17 日から、住所・電話・FAX 番号が変わります。
〒 170-0005　東京都豊島区南大塚 2-32-4
Tel: 03-5395-4811　Fax: 03-5395-4812

印刷・製本　（株）サンニチ印刷
製版　エバーベスト・プリンティング（株）

©2003　P・I・E BOOKS

Printed in Japan
ISBN4-89444-239-6 C3070